MW00588486

# Pioneers, Prisoners, and Peace Pipes

*True Stories about*
*Settlers, Soldiers, Indians, and Outlaws*
*on the Pennsylvania Frontier*

# JOHN L. MOORE

SUNBURY
PRESS

**Mechanicsburg, Pennsylvania  USA**

9/8/2018
R.L.S.

Published by Sunbury Press, Inc.
50 West Main Street
Mechanicsburg, Pennsylvania 17055

**www.sunburypress.com**

Although the people whose experiences are chronicled in this book are dead, their stories survive in letters, diaries, journals, official reports, depositions, interrogations, examinations, minutes, and memoirs. These sources are quoted liberally. An occasional ellipsis indicates where words or phrases have been omitted. Punctuation and spelling have been modernized.

For information about special discounts for bulk purchases, please contact Sunbury Press Orders Dept. at (855) 338-8359 or orders@sunburypress.com.

To request one of our authors for speaking engagements or book signings, please contact Sunbury Press Publicity Dept. at publicity@sunburypress.com.

ISBN: 978-1-62006-514-3 (Trade Paperback)
Library of Congress Control Number: 2014956353

FIRST SUNBURY PRESS EDITION: November 2014

*Product of the United States of America*
0  1  1  2  3  5  8  13  21  34  55

Set in Bookman Old Style
Designed by Lawrence Knorr
Cover by Lawrence Knorr
Cover Art "Escape" by Andrew Knez, Jr.
Edited by Janice Rhayem

*Continue the Enlightenment!*

# JOHN L. MOORE's

## FRONTIER PENNSYLVANIA SERIES

*Bows, Bullets, & Bears*
*Cannons, Cattle, & Campfires*
*Forts, Forests, & Flintlocks*
*Pioneers, Prisoners, & Peace Pipes*
*Rivers, Raiders, & Renegades*
*Settlers, Soldiers, & Scalps*
*Traders, Travelers, & Tomahawks*
*Warriors, Wampum, & Wolves*

# Author's Note on Quotations

I have taken a journalist's approach to writing about the people whose lives and experiences are chronicled in this book. Long dead, they nonetheless speak to us through the many letters, diaries, journals, official reports, depositions, interrogations, examinations, minutes, and memoirs that they left behind.

Whenever possible, I have presented the people I have written about in their own words. My intent is to allow the reader a sense of immediacy with historical figures who lived two or more centuries ago. To accomplish this, I have occasionally omitted phrases or sentences from quotations, and I have employed an ellipsis (...) to indicate where I have done so. In some instances, I have modernized punctuation; and in others, spelling has been modernized.

John L. Moore
Northumberland, PA
October 2014

# Dedication

For Dan, Melody and Andy.

# Acknowledgments

My thanks to my son, Andrew R. Moore, for suggesting the title, and to my wife, Jane E. Pritchard-Moore, for editing the manuscript. Thanks also to Robert B. Swift for many valuable suggestions, to Thomas Brucia for proofreading the manuscript, to Kathleen A. Szautner for translating Michael La Chauvignerie's letter to his father from French to English, to Johann F. Szautner for translating the German verse on George Row's tombstone into English, and to Chuck Dixon of Dixon's Muzzle-loading Shop for offering a plausible suggestion about why Richard Bard might have placed tow in the pan of his flintlock pistol before hanging the loaded weapon on the wall of his cabin.

# Messengers Find Fear on the Trail

*November 1755*

In July 1755 Indian warriors and French soldiers defeated the British soldiers who had marched over the mountains from Virginia with Gen. Edward Braddock to capture the French forts along the Ohio and Allegheny rivers. Three months later—during the autumn of 1755—Indian war parties began raiding Pennsylvania settlements along the Susquehanna River.

Brother Joseph Spangenberg, the Moravian bishop at Bethlehem, realized that missionaries sent by his church into the frontier were probably exposed to danger, so he sent two messengers, Brothers John Schmick and Henry Fry, into the forests to ask some friendly Shawnee Indians for their help in recalling the missionaries.

Bethlehem was a small religious community built on a hill overlooking the Lehigh River about ten miles west of the newly settled village of Easton at the Lehigh's confluence with the Delaware River. A major north-south Indian trail passed through Bethlehem, and Schmick and Fry, traveling on foot, followed this trail when they left Bethlehem on Thursday, November 6, 1755. They headed north toward Wyoming, at modern Wilkes-Barre, where the Shawnee Indians had a town along the Susquehanna River's North Branch. They took the Lehigh Path, which joined the Lehigh River at the gap near present-day Palmerton, and stopped at the Moravian mission of Gnadenhutten, situated at the confluence of the Lehigh and Mahoning Creek. A dozen missionaries, European emigrants, ran the mission, which had attracted several hundred

1

*August Gottlieb "Brother Joseph" Spangenberg (1704–1792)*

Native American residents. The modern communities of Lehighton and Weissport occupy the site.

Once north of the mission, Fry and Schmick walked as quickly as they could, but because their route crossed rugged mountains, the trip took four days. Although there was constant danger of meeting hostile Indian war parties or even walking into an ambush, the travelers noted in their journal, "We had no gun with us."

As they walked north on Sunday, November 9, they encountered a solitary traveler—an "Indian who had a bundle of skins on his back and a gun in his hand"—who was headed south.

"As soon as he saw us, (he) cried out in a great fright, 'Who are you?' We answered, 'Good friends,'" the Moravians reported. "We then asked him where he came from and where he would go."

The Indian replied that he was coming down from Wyoming, bound for Gnadenhutten. "When he came near us, we saw that he trembled with fear," Schmick and Fry reported. "He then asked us where we came from, and, hearing that we came from Gnadenhutten, he shook hands friendly with us and laid his gun down by a tree and lit his pipe, and asked how the Indians in Gnadenhutten did, and if all was quiet and peaceable there."

As the Indian smoked his pipe, the Europeans reported that "all was well and peaceable" in the mission settlement. The Indian said that he had a brother at Gnadenhutten, whom he intended to visit. "He was a Delaware, and Schmick spoke Delaware with him," the Moravians said. The Moravians soon resumed their trek, and the Indian continued walking south.

When traveling, Indians frequently used a strap fashioned of leather or tree bark to carry goods on their backs. Some hours later "as we went up a mountain, we observed a bearskin with flesh in it, tied up with a carrying band, hanging on a tree by the way."

3

They kept on walking, crossed the mountain's summit, and were descending when another Indian, headed north on horseback, overtook them. The man "told us that the Indian whom the flesh belonged to was afraid of us and had run into the woods to hide ..." As for himself, the horseman said he had been down to Gnadenhutten and was now going home to Wyoming.

The Moravians camped along the trail that night. "The next day in going down the Wyoming Mountain, we saw an Indian before us with a bearskin and a deerskin and some flesh on his back and a gun in his hand. ... As soon as he observed us, (he) walked so fast that we could not overtake him in two miles' distance. But being then a good way before us, he rested his burden against a tree, and seeing we had no gun with us, he stayed till we came up with him. We then asked him where he lived. He said at Wyoming and so we passed on and left him. He was a Delaware and looked frightened."

Around noon on Monday, November 10, the messengers crossed the North Branch of the Susquehanna River and soon after reached the Indian town of Wyoming, where many Shawnee had settled. When the Indians heard that white people had come into the village, "they all stood in their doors to see us and saluted us." Fry and Schmick presently arrived at the home of Paxinosa, the Shawnee chief. He and the other Indian leaders welcomed the Moravians warmly. The messengers explained that Bishop Spangenberg requested their help in retrieving Marcus Kiefer, the blacksmith assigned to the Moravian mission at Shamokin (present-day Sunbury).

Such an undertaking could be perilous. Located at the confluence of the North and West branches of the Susquehanna River, Shamokin was nearly seventy miles down the North Branch, and the Shawnee leaders suspected that many of the Indians living there had decided to side with the French. Paxinosa and another influential Shawnee, Jonathan, told Schmick and Fry that they had recently been summoned to Shamokin. They had arrived to find "that Indians there were convened to a treaty, where a French Mohawk Indian gave a string of wampum and addressed the other Indians."

The Mohawk told them, "Your grandfather ..., the French king, sends you word that I (the king) intend to come down (the Susquehanna River) with 1,500 men ... But do not you be afraid for I do not design to hurt you, but only the white people like myself." The Mohawk cautioned, however, that any Indians who stood too close to the Pennsylvania colonists could be injured by the "broad sharp hatchet" that the French soldiers would bring.

Despite the danger, the Shawnees decided to do as the Moravians asked even though Paxinosa and Jonathan explained, "We are old. We can't travel well." They explained that younger men would carry out the request. As Fry reported later, "Paxinosa said, 'I will send my son,' and Jonathan said, 'I am willing to go with him and to fetch the brother to Wyoming, if he is yet alive.'"

The rescue party set out on horseback the next day, which was Tuesday, November 11. They carried a letter that Bishop Spangenberg had written to the blacksmith directing him "to leave the (mission) house and things ... and go forthwith" to Wyoming with the Shawnees. Before they left, Paxinosa gave them specific instructions. They were to follow the Wyoming Path that ran along the river's western side as far as the small Delaware town at present-day Catawissa, located on the eastern shore. They were to ford the river and enquire as to "how it was at Shamokin—if the French were there, as they in Wyoming had been informed, erecting a fort."

Were the Delawares at Catawissa to warn them of danger at Shamokin, the Shawnees should continue until they reached a point about six miles north of Shamokin. They should leave their horses and "go on in the night to Shamokin and to go to the brother's house and get him away in the night."

As it turned out, the French were not building a fort at Shamokin. The two Shawnees reached the Indian town without incident and quickly found the blacksmith hiding in the home of a friendly Indian family. Kiefer readily left with them and got to Wyoming and, eventually, to Bethlehem safely.

In the mean time, John Schmick and Henry Fry returned to Bethlehem and reported to the Moravian leaders there the facts, observations and anecdotes on which this article is based. An official copy of the Schmick-Fry chronicle—which Timothy Horsfield, the justice of the peace at Bethlehem, wrote on November 15, 1755, after interviewing the travelers—was sent to Gov. Robert Hunter Morris in Philadelphia. The missive appears among the thousands of documents that comprise the Pennsylvania Archives.

# Hostile Encounter in the Minisinks

*July 1756*

In William Penn's time, an ancient Indian trail, known today as the Minsi Path, ran north from Philadelphia through Bethlehem across the Blue Mountain and on to present-day Stroudsburg. From there, it coursed along the Delaware River, passing through such modern Pennsylvania places as Shawnee On Delaware and Bushkill before swinging east at Port Jervis, New York, and heading for the Hudson River at Kingston, NY.

As white settlers moved into the Upper Delaware Valley, they called the region north of the Delaware Water Gap by its Indian name—the Minisinks. Over time, the newcomers improved the Indian trail so they could drive farm wagons over it. When the French and Indian War began in 1755, native raiders came into the valley, burned many farms, and killed many inhabitants.

In December 1755, Indian raids on white settlements in the Pocono Mountains prompted frontier farmers and Pennsylvania troops to organize defenses and erect fortifications. At present-day Bushkill lived a frontiersman named James Hyndshaw, who in January 1756 became a lieutenant in the Pennsylvania Regiment. Hyndshaw's house stood on the bank of Bushkill Creek, about a quarter mile up from where the creek entered the Delaware River. The location was strategic: the building stood along a road that followed the river and provided a land route to settlements at modern Shawnee On Delaware, just north of the Delaware Water Gap. Reacting to the outbreak of hostilities, Hyndshaw, his

*Minsi Path, South (from* Indian Paths
of Pennsylvania *by Paul A. W.
Wallace, pg. 103)*

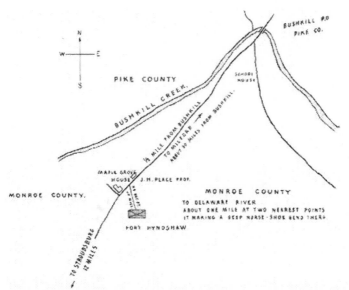

*Map depicting the site of Fort Hyndshaw near Bushkill.
(courtesy of the Monroe County Historical Association)*

neighbors, and members of the frontier soldiers hastily erected a log wall around the house, which they named Fort Hyndshaw. When James Young, the Pennsylvania Regiment's commissary officer, visited the post in June, he reported that he took "a good plain road from Dupues" (modern Shawnee On Delaware) in lower Monroe County.

Young noted that he saw many farms "along the way, but all deserted and the houses chiefly burnt."

When he reached the fort, he found that its site was "clear all round for 300 yards," and that the fort itself was a square, with sides 70 feet long and "very slightly stockaded. I gave some directions to alter the bastions, which at present are of little use."

Young added that Lieutenant Hyndshaw had a force of twenty-five men at the post.

As summer deepened, white farmers continued to work their lands despite fears that Indian war parties might be lurking in the woods. In mid-July Indians ambushed white travelers along the Minisinks Road and killed four. After that, the farmers arranged for military patrols to guard them as they worked in their fields. It was following one of these work parties that Captain John Van Etten, who had become the fort's commander, wrote to Governor Robert Morris on July 24.

Two days earlier, the captain reported, settlers living about fifteen miles above the fort had requested protection. "I sent a sergeant with four men up there to guard some farmers in their harvest, and as they came to the field, some of the company was behind and they halloed to one another and after the second hallo, there was an Indian (who) halloed at some distance toward the mountain and inquired for the captain."

Van Etten wasn't present, but his brother, Johannis Van Etten, was, and in a loud voice he replied to the Indian, "I am the man."

"Come you to us," the Indian said in broken English.

Van Etten did, and as the soldier approached, the Indian asked if he was alone.

"He said yes, but made a sign for Sgt. Cole and the company to stay back," the captain reported.

At this point, Van Etten asked the Indian to come to him, but the Indian declined and said, "Come you more up the mountain."

Van Etten did, "and they met and shook hands together."

The soldier asked the Indian what he wanted. "He said to know if they were busy to work in the harvest and how it went."

Then Van Etten asked him to go down with him to the house, but the Indian declined, and explained that "the Indians have done so much mischief here last winter that he was afraid to come down."

Van Etten insisted. "If you are a friend," he said, "you need not be afraid for you shall not be hurt."

But the Indian refused, and said that he intended to "return that day again to Wigwamonck (Wyoming)."

"Then Van Etten asked him if he would drink a dram with him, and he said, yes, and ... Van Etten sent for the bottle and drank to him and asked him from whence he came.

"He said from Wywamonck. Van Etten told him he lied."

The Indian responded by confessing that he came from Tioga, a Delaware town on the North Branch of the Susquehanna River at present-day Athens.

Van Etten asked how many prisoners were there, and the Indian replied that four had been there, but were gone.

As they spoke, Van Etten realized that at least two other Indians were nearby and told the man "to call the other two Indians to come to him if you are friends and you shall not be hurt."

The Indian did as requested, and a young Indian came, but the other one would not.

Van Etten pointedly asked the man about four whites who had been murdered the week before on Minisinks Road. "But when he (Van Etten) talked with him about that, he (the Indian) was for going away and kept himself well guarded with his gun while he was surrounded."

Van Etten and the Indian agreed that Van Etten should go with the young Indian and bring in the other Indian. The two had walked about a hundred yards from the company, when Van Etten suddenly ordered the young warrior to "call to the other Indian."

He said he would, but instead he looked back and ran off, "whereupon Van Etten fired upon him." Van Etten's gun apparently was loaded with scatter shot, and the bulk of the pellets must have missed the running Indian, because, in the captain's words, "only the swan shot hit him."

The shot startled the Indian who had remained with the patrol. "Hearing the gun, (the Indian) forced himself through the company and run off, whereupon they fired nine guns upon him and killed him and took off his scalp," the captain reported.

As this happened, the young Indian and the warrior who had remained on the mountain got away.

# Provincial Soldiers Keep 'a Bad Lookout'

*August 1756*

The Swatara Creek drains the mountains and valleys northeast of Harrisburg. Below the mountains, it flows southward across rolling countryside, emptying into the Susquehanna River at Middletown. A pioneer named Adam Reed had built a log cabin along the Swatara in present-day Lebanon County, a little west of the village of Ono. In time, he became a justice of the peace. When the Indian raids began in October 1755, he helped organize armed patrols to range along the Blue Mountain between the Susquehanna and Schuylkill rivers.

Reed remained active in the colony's defense, and August 7, 1756, found him writing to Edward Shippen, another man deeply involved in protecting the settlements, about an episode that involved soldiers from Fort Manada, located about a dozen miles west of Reed's fortified home. A small log stockade built in early 1756 along the eastern branch of Manada Creek, this post, which was also known as Brown's Fort, was situated roughly half a mile from Manada Gap, which it guarded. The fort stood about fifteen miles northeast of present-day Harrisburg.

One of the soldiers garrisoned at Brown's Fort, Jacob Elles, or Ellis, had a farm a short distance north of the gap. Few Indians had been spotted in recent weeks, and Ellis, "having some wheat growing at his place, prevailed with his officer for some of ye men to help him cut a little ..."

The farm was about three miles away from Manada Fort, and Captain Friedrich Schmitt, whose garrison

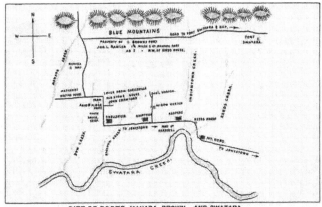

SITE OF FORTS MANADA, BROWN, AND SWATARA.

consisted of twenty-one men, allowed ten of them to go to the Ellis homestead.

Ellis and his nine companions "went, set guards round and fell to work," Reed reported. By ten o'clock, they had reaped down one side of the wheat field, reversed course, "and went to the head to begin again and before they had all well begun, three Indians crept to ye fence just at their back and all three at one panel of the fence fired upon them, killed their corporal dead. ... Another (soldier) that was standing with his gun in one hand and a bottle in ye other was wounded. His left arm is broke in two places so that his gun fell."

The Indians quickly realized that the reapers had left "their arms about half way down (the field) at a large tree. ... They did not load their guns but leaped over ye fence into the middle of them and one of them left his gun behind him without ye fence."

Painted and decorated for war, the warriors gave the war cry, which Reed said was "a terrible halloo." To the terrified soldiers, each attacker looked more like "ye Devil than an Indian."

Several soldiers ran to the tree and got their guns. "As three of them stood behind ye tree with their arms,

14

ye Indian that came in wanting his gun came within a few yards of them and took up the wounded soldier's gun," Reed said. The Indian was preparing to shoot another man when a soldier "fired at him so that he dropped the gun. The Indians fled and in going off, two soldiers stood about a rod (sixteen feet) apart. An Indian run through betwixt them. They both fired at him, yet he went off clear."

In an instant, all three Indians had jumped over the fence and were sprinting towards the woods. "A soldier fired at one of them, upon which he stooped a little," Reed reported. But the warrior kept on going, "and so went all three off."

The soldiers quickly decided against pursuing their attackers. Instead, they hid the body of the corporal and were about to head back to the gap and Brown's Fort when suddenly they heard a gunshot and immediately thereafter an Indian giving the scalp-halloo, or scalp yell. The sounds came from the direction in which the war party had gone.

The nine men marched the three miles back to the fort in a hurry. When they got there, they learned that James Brown, a soldier who lived in the fort, was missing.

Captain Schmitt decided to send a patrol back to the Ellis farm to retrieve the corporal's body. "The lieutenant went out with more men and brought in the dead man, but still Brown was missing," Reed wrote afterward. "I heard shooting that night. I went up next morning with some hands."

Schmitt had also sent out patrols, and word came "that they had found James Brown killed and scalped," Reed said.

"I went over with them to bring him home. He was killed with that last shot ... His gun, his shoes and his jacket (were) carried off. The soldiers that found him told me that they tracked the three Indians to the second mountain and they found one of the Indians' guns a little from Brown's corpse broke to pieces as she had been good for little. They showed me where ye

15

*Edward Shippen (1729-1806)*

Indians fired through ye fence and it was full 11 yards to where the man lay dead. Ye rising ground above ye field was clear of standing timber and the grubes (brush) low, so that they had kept a bad lookout."

Adam Reed ended his letter to Edward Shippen on a pessimistic note: "We have almost lost all hopes of anything but to move off and lose our crops we have reaped with so much difficulty."

# Bushwackers in the Woods at Bethlehem

*November 1756*

As the frontier war progressed, many Christian Indians who had lived at Gnadenhutten and other Moravian missions came to Bethlehem for sanctuary.

If Bethlehem residents welcomed and sheltered the converts, many of the region's non-Moravians weren't nearly as hospitable. For instance, on November 29, 1756, magistrate Timothy Horsfield reported the misfortune of an Indian man living at Bethlehem. To understand Horsfield's account, it is important to know that Indian warriors plucked all their hair except for a topknot called a scalp lock. The peaceful Indian men at Bethlehem let their hair grow to their shoulders so that everyone could see that they weren't warriors.

"One of our Indians," the magistrate wrote, "was in the woods a small distance from Bethlehem with his gun, hoping to meet with a deer." Luckless, the hunter was walking along a forest path that led to Bethlehem when he met two white men. To show that he wasn't a warrior, "he saluted by taking off his hat," Horsfield said. He walked past the men, but "he had not gone far when he heard a gun fired and the bullet whistled near by him." Terrified, the Indian started "running through the thick bushes." His gun got caught on a branch and discharged. "He dropped it, his hat, blanket, etc. and came home much frighted."

*Timothy Horsfield, painted by Valentine Haidt. Historical Society of Western Pennsylvania.*

# Boy Soldier Nearly Starves in the Woods

*Summer 1757*

Michael La Chauvignerie was a sixteen-year-old French soldier who left his home in Canada during the summer of 1756, bound for the Ohio country. Michael didn't know it as he left Montreal and sailed up the St. Lawrence River, but he had embarked on the first leg of a prolonged and complicated adventure that would take him to Philadelphia and, ultimately, to the Caribbean Sea.

Details are sparse of the youth's journey from Montreal to the Allegheny River Valley in what is now Western Pennsylvania. The Allegheny and the Monongahela join at present-day Pittsburgh to form the Ohio River. In 1754, the French had erected Fort Duquesne at the confluence, and in 1755 an officer known as the Sieur de La Chauvignerie began building a smaller post, Fort Machault, on the Allegheny about seventy-five miles above Fort Duquesne. This officer was Michael's father, and Michael was soon part of the garrison at Fort Machault, which his father commanded. Despite his youth, Michael had attained the rank of ensign by 1757, and his father began sending him out with Indian war parties headed for Pennsylvania.

To understand Michael's story, it is necessary to know a little about the conflict then raging between the English and the Native Americans and between the English and the French in present-day Western Pennsylvania. In 1757 the Ohio Valley was a disputed territory. Its chief inhabitants were Indians, many of them Delawares who had abandoned their traditional homelands along the Hudson, Raritan, Delaware,

Lehigh, and Schuylkill Rivers in southeastern New York, New Jersey, and eastern Pennsylvania. These regions were now occupied by thousands of immigrants from Europe. Many of these Indians regarded Western Pennsylvania as a place of refuge, but it had become a land of conflict. France and England each claimed it.

In 1755 a British army led by Gen. Edward Braddock pushed north and west from Virginia to expel French soldiers who in recent years had come down from Canada and erected a chain of forts along the Allegheny and Ohio Rivers. In July, French troops and Indian warriors had defeated Braddock's army, and a conflict known as the French and Indian War had begun.

As the elderly Indian speaker Ackowanothie, representing the Delawares and other Ohio tribes, some years later explained to Conrad Weiser, the Pennsylvania Indian agent: "Your nation always showed an eagerness to settle our lands. Cunning as they were, they always encouraged a number of poor people to settle upon our lands. We protested against it several times, but without any redress or help. We pitied the poor people; we did not care to make use of force, and indeed some of those people were very good people, and as hospitable as we Indians ... but after all we lost our hunting ground, for where one of those people settled, like pigeons, a thousand more would settle, so that we at last offered to sell it ... and so it went on 'til we at last jumped over (the) Allegheny hills and settled on the waters of Ohio. Here we thought ourselves happy. We had plenty of game, a rich and large country, and a country that the Most High had created for the poor Indians, and not for the white people."

The years passed, and one day the Indians had been startled to learn that the king of England had "given away that land to a parcel of covetous gentlemen from Virginia, called the Ohio Company, who came immediately and offered to build forts among us, no doubt, to make themselves master of our lands, and make slaves of us, to which we could not agree," Ackowanothie said.

When Braddock's troops crossed the Alleghenies and approached Fort Duquesne during the spring and summer of 1755, the Indians who had once lived in eastern Pennsylvania sided with the French and took up arms against the English. As Ackowanothie explained, "We can drive away the French when we please. They have even promised to go off when we pleased, provided we would not suffer the English to take possession of the lands ... (But) we can never drive you off, you are such a numerous people; and that makes us afraid of your army."

Michael La Chauvignerie's father appears frequently in the story of this conflict. He built the log outpost—Fort Machault—at the confluence of French Creek and the Allegheny, where present-day Franklin stands. The creek ran a crooked northerly course toward Lake Erie, and French military expeditions coming down from Canada sailed along the lake as far as modern Erie, then portaged the short distance to French Creek and, using small boats called bateaux, came down the creek to the river. The Allegheny twisted and turned as it flowed southwesterly to join the Monongahela and form the Ohio. In 1754 the French evicted English traders from Virginia who had fortified a storehouse at the confluence. In erecting a defense of their own—Fort Duquesne, the French soldiers used hewn logs and posts that the Virginians had fashioned for use in their own structure.

### Fort Machault

Fort Machault stood on the Allegheny River's west bank and was often referred to as "the fort at Venango." Outfitted with swivel guns, its shape was that of a square. Each corner sported a bastion, and the fort's gate opened toward the river. One French colonial official, in a January 1759 report, described

21

*An artist's rendition of the French Fort Machault and the barracks erected nearby.*

the outpost as strong enough to withstand an attack of musket fire, "but cannon would quickly demolish it."

With Fort Machault erected and garrisoned, several Indian villages sprang up in its vicinity. Many of these Indians were Delawares, and French soldiers reported that many belonged to the Tribe of the Wolves.

Lieutenant La Chauvignerie began his effort to build Fort Machault in 1755, but encountered a variety of difficulties. He lacked sufficient soldiers and horses to transport suitable logs to the fort site. He also needed a military engineer to supervise construction. He made this clear in a July 1755 letter to his superior, Captain Claude-Pierre Pecaudy, sieur de Contrecoeur, who commanded at Fort Duquesne. La Chauvignerie reported that he had selected and largely cleared the site for the fort, but he also emphasized that the soldiers assigned to work on the project needed to be "accompanied by an officer capable of directing these kinds of works and laying the plans for them ..." A month later he informed his superior that even though no engineer was present to supervise the fort's construction, he had kept his troops busy in felling timber in the nearby forest. "Almost all the wood is cut and ready to haul," La Chauvignerie reported.

By mid-1756, reports reaching the English settlements contained news that the French had built Fort Machault and had equipped it with cannon. An English prisoner named William Marshall spent a week at Venango during the summer of 1756. Marshall eventually escaped and made his way back to the English colonies where he described Lieutenant La Chauvignerie as "a fat, jolly man with one eye ..."

The new post was intended mainly to serve as a supply depot for Fort Duquesne, which was further down the Allegheny, but its commander also used it as a base for Indian raids against the Pennsylvania colony. With the fort finally constructed, La Chauvignerie began sending war parties to the Susquehanna River Valley far to the east. In February 1757, for instance, a raiding party of fourteen Indians and six French Canadians spied on Fort Augusta, which the Pennsylvania Regiment had built the previous summer along the Susquehanna River at modern Sunbury. The raiders returned to Machault and reported that they had killed and scalped two Pennsylvania soldiers within sight of the fort.

The troops belonging to the garrison at Fort Machault included the lieutenant's son, who was now seventeen. Roughly a year had passed since Michael had left Montreal. The teenager seems to have been spoiling for adventure, because his father sent him out with Indian war parties several times during the summer of 1757. He was part of a war party that left Fort Machault on September 11, headed for the Pennsylvania settlements more than two hundred miles away. At first, there were thirty-three Indians on the expedition, with only a few Frenchmen going along.

In recounting the adventure later, the younger La Chauvignerie didn't specify the exact route the warriors took, but did report that they traveled "about 14 days over a very mountainous country," and eventually "they passed over Susquehanna about two days journey below Fort Augusta, as the Indians told him, at a place where he saw some peach trees and the ruins of a house with some clear land around it."

It's possible that the war party took a round-about route from Venango to Frankstown following the Frankstown Path, then swung east along the Juniata

23

Path and crossed the Susquehanna at present-day Dalmatia. Once across the river, the Indians may have proceeded east until they encountered the Tulpehocken Path, which took them south to the frontier settlements in northwestern Berks County.

Although lengthy, the round-about route—which followed well-established Indian trails—had the virtue of bypassing the forts at Sunbury, Dauphin, Halifax, and Harrisburg and of avoiding patrols organized by these outposts to range the trails and watch for signs of war parties.

### The Susquehanna

Although La Chauvignerie had set out with a sizable force, he had reached the Susquehanna with a much smaller number of warriors. As he said later, "after traveling about 14 days ... they met another party of Indians returning from war, with three prisoners, ... two young women and one man, ... and had taken one scalp ... They gave the man prisoner to the Indians of his party, and ... all his party returned save 12 who came with him."

This smaller force crossed the Susquehanna in late September and traveled for another three days before reaching the cabins and barns that the English and German farmers had built in the valleys of the Blue Mountains, north of Lancaster and Reading.

The Indians and their French companions became cautious travelers. La Chauvignerie said later "that they made no fires in the night except at some of the many deserted houses which they saw, especially among the hills; that they buried the fires when they went away and took great care to make no noise."

In time, the war party came to a house whose occupants had not fled. The Indians raided the structure, and quickly overpowered the white people inside it—five small children. The Indians decided to take the children—"four girls and one boy," according to La Chauvignerie. Neither father nor mother was at home, and the attackers theorized that "they might be at some neighbor's house."

The warriors ransacked the cabin and "took some clothes for the children and some provisions and several other things for themselves." The war party stayed about half an hour at this cabin, then left.

The parents of the children were not far away. They had gone to a nearby meadow for a load of hay. They returned to the cabin shortly after the Indians had departed and were horrified to find all the children gone and the cabin plundered. Soon after, the editor of the Pennsylvania Gazette received and published a letter dated Oct. 1 that told of the raid. "The Indians took from the house what they thought most valuable and destroyed what they could not take away," the newspaper reported.

Another newspaper, that of Christopher Saur, printed a similar but more detailed account of this letter: The newspaper reported that Peter Wampler, who had emigrated from Germany aboard the ship Lydia in 1741, "and his wife were in the fields, bringing in a wagon with hay. The Indians took five children off with them, four girls and one boy. The smallest child is scarce a year old and cannot walk yet." Eager for booty, the warriors quickly gathered up "all they could carry," then vandalized the cabin. "The rest they destroyed," the letter writer said. When the Wamplers returned to the house, they discovered their children gone, possessions stolen and house vandalized—for the Indians had "scattered the flour, spilled the honey, broke the pots and windows and tore up the beds."

The Wamplers never saw the children again.

The raid was one of a number of incidents that terrorized the back country farmers that autumn. "Murder is committed almost every day," Conrad Weiser said in an October 3 letter to Richard Peters, secretary to the governor. Weiser, who lived at present-day Womelsdorf, was both a justice of the peace and a lieutenant colonel in the Pennsylvania Regiment.

"There never was such a consternation among the people," he told Peters. "They must now leave their houses again, with their barns full of grain. Five children have been carried off last Friday."

It was Michael La Chauvignerie who provided details of the raiding party's excursion across the frontier settlements. Even as the parents loaded their hay wagon and drove it toward the barn, the Indians had started a hasty retreat, taking the children to the west. They came to another homestead several miles away, and the warriors "took some horses ... and put the children on them. (They) passed a great many houses which appeared to be deserted, (and) saw geese and fowl about them," the young soldier reported.

Satisfied with their prisoners and plunder, the Indians decided to return to the Ohio country. Eager to elude any pursuers who might try to rescue the children, they headed west at a fast speed. It had taken three days to reach the settlements after crossing the river, but the return trip required only two days to get to the Susquehanna.

### Lost Rations

After crossing the river, the Indians continued walking at a rapid pace for several days, traveling in single-file. Late in the afternoon of the third day following the crossing, La Chauvignerie encountered trouble. Members of the war party had limited rations, and he had carried his portion tucked in his shirt. As Michael walked rapidly along the forest trail, his food had fallen out. He said later that he had "dropped a piece of bread (and) stopped to look for it. ... In the time he was searching for it, his party of Indians got so far ahead of him that he could not overtake or make them hear him."

If the Indians realized he was missing, they didn't wait for him to catch up or send anyone back to find him. For his part, the young soldier spent two days trying to find his companions, and then—"being afraid of starving"—Michael La Chauvignerie reversed course and once again headed for the Pennsylvania settlements, this time intending to surrender at a fort in the hope that the soldiers might feed him.

After crossing the Susquehanna for the third time in two weeks, Michael followed forest paths that took him to the southeast. Trying to stay close to the war party's original route, he walked down long valleys and climbed steep and rocky mountains. At one point, where the Swatara Creek flowed through a gap in the Second Mountain, the trail became less than two feet wide. The path that Michael most likely took negotiated this gap by means of a narrow ledge across the face of a cliff on the gap's east side. Interstate 81 now passes through the gap, which is located just north of the Schuylkill County village of Ravine.

La Chauvignerie's solitary trek through the forest lasted a week, but at last, the youth reached the settlements, and he "delivered himself up at Fort Henry the seventh day after he lost himself ..., which he chose to do rather than starve in the woods ..."

Troops garrisoned at Fort Henry, located along the Tulpehocken Path at the foot of the Blue Mountain near modern Bethel, captured the Frenchman as he approached a house near the fort on October 15. The soldiers soon took him to Conrad Weiser's home about ten miles away.

Writing from Reading on October 16, Weiser relayed news of Michael's capture to Gov. William Denny:

[Ensign Kern] informed me that ... a French deserter or spy came down the hill near Fort Henry and made toward Deitrick Six's house, which, the sentry of the fort observing, acquainted the commanding officer ... who sent an officer and two soldiers to seize and bring him into the fort ... I ordered by express my son, Samuel, who commanded the fort on Swatara, to march with a ranging party with all possible speed and care and take the said prisoner and convey him safe to my house in

*Hand-drawn portrait of Conrad Weiser, artist unknown.*

Heidelberg, where he arrived safe with the prisoner about noon yesterday."

### Interrogation

"I examined the prisoner by such an interpreter as I could get, but thought fit to bring him down hither (Reading) to have a more full examination by the assistance of Captain Oswald and Mr. James Read and accordingly came here with him last night."

Weiser took Michael to Reading the next day for a formal interrogation. Aiding Weiser in examining the prisoner were:

— James Read, Esq., who, like Weiser, was a justice of the peace;

— Captain Thomas Oswald, commanding officer of a company in the Royal American Regiment. The unit was stationed in Reading.

— Ensign Shaw, a member of Oswald's company.

Two other members of Oswald's company were also present: Lieutenant Brigstock and Ensign Hart.

As the interrogation progressed, Weiser, a German who spoke English with a German accent, questioned the prisoner in English. La Chauvignerie responded in French, which Captain Oswald, Read and Ensign Shaw interpreted.

A brief but verbatim transcript of the interview survives:

Weiser: "What prisoners did you meet on your expedition into this country?"

LC: "One man and two women, the eldest woman about 20 years old, and the other a little younger, whom I took to be sisters. I believe they were all English."

W: "Where did you meet them, and how long after you left Fort Machault?"

LC: "I cannot say where, but I left Fort Machault the 11th September last, and met them about 18 days after, and before I passed the River Susquehanna."

29

## JOHN L. MOORE

W: "How long after you met the prisoners did you pass Susquehanna?"

LC: "I cannot remember."

W: "How many days after your passing Susquehanna did you make any prisoners?"

LC: "Three days after passing Susquehanna we took five children."

W: "How many days after your making these prisoners did you continue with your party?"

LC: "Five days, and then I lost them."

W: "How long did you remain alone in the woods afterwards?"

LC: "Seven days. But I may have forgot a day as I was in great distress."

W: "What was the name of the other French man who was of your party?"

LC: "Le Jardin. I don't know his Christian name. "

W: "What Indian chief, besides Maconse, was with you?"

LC: "La Grande Terre, who was the Indian commander, Maconse being a guide for us. Maconse has a brother in this part of the country."

W: "Who commanded the party which you met with prisoners as you came down?"

LC: "I don't know."

W: "Was [sic] you ever on another expedition into this province?"

LC: "About four months ago, I came with seven Indians under my command on this side Susquehanna, and having passed two mountains they killed and scalped a man. By his dress, I took him to be a German, and soon after I was coming again into the same part of the country with five Indians, but being lame, they concealed me on the way at a small Indian town on Susquehanna lest I should be taken. They continued their journey, and five days after returned to me with two German children, prisoners, a boy and a girl, about 12 or 13 years of age."

W: "How many captives has your father at his fort, who are servants to him?"

LC: "Three. Two were presented to him and one he bought of the Indians. He had two others, one of whom he bought and the other was presented to him. These two he has sent to Montreal. The Indians have a very great number of prisoners, but they can scarce be prevailed with to part with any of them."

W: "What sort of fort is Machault?"

LC: "It is a fort of wood, filled up with earth. It has bastions and six wall pieces, or swivel guns, and the whole works take up about two acres of ground."

W: "What number of regular soldiers, Canadians and Indians is there at the fort?"

LC: "50 regulars and 40 Canadians. No Indians are there, but (they) pass and repass to and from a little town about seven leagues west from Fort Machault, called Ticastoroga. They are of the tribe of the Wolf."

W: "How many men are at Niagara?"

LC: "Two battalions."

Michael La Chauvignerie readily gave up significant intelligence to his interrogators. Colonial authorities examined him at length and gathered a good deal of detailed information about French military defenses and troop strength. He told them, for instance, that when he had visited Fort Duquesne the previous June, he had noted "about 20 cannon ..., some mortars, four bastions and a dry ditch" around the fort's log walls. He reported "that there were about 1,500 men at Fort Duquesne, of which 500 are regulars and the rest are employed in the carrying of provisions" between the far-flung French posts along the Ohio and its tributaries. And then La Chauvignerie made a statement that becomes curious in light of his strong and recent fear of starving in the forest. "There were," he said, "a great number of English prisoners at

## JOHN L. MOORE

Fort Duquesne, but they are constantly sending them away to Montreal, that they are not used as slaves but as prisoners of war when they arrive there and are fed as the soldiers are."

His willingness to talk about military matters made the young man something of an official curiosity, and he was taken to Philadelphia where William Allen, Esq., the chief justice of the Province of Pennsylvania, questioned him. Part of the interest in the youth may have been that he readily identified himself as the son of the Sieur de La Chauvignerie, the commandant at Fort Machault.

Much of this article is based on the transcript of Allen's interrogation of La Chauvignerie. The document is dated October 26, 1757, which means that in a little more than six weeks, the fortunes of war took the talkative young soldier from a remote post along the French military route between Montreal and Fort Duquesne to Philadelphia, then the capital of Pennsylvania, and encounters with top level officials of the colony.

One detail in the transcript of Allen's interrogation dealt with the prisoner himself. "It is about 14 months since he left Montreal," the chief justice reported.

By late 1757, Indian war parties had taken hundreds of white people from the Pennsylvania settlements, and Pennsylvania authorities pressed La Chauvignerie for an account of what had happened to them. In his interview with the chief justice, Michael reported "that the Indians keep many of the prisoners amongst them, chiefly young people whom they adopt and bring up in their own way, and ... those prisoners whom the Indians keep with them become so well satisfied and pleased with the way of living that they don't care to leave them ..."

As La Chauvignerie told it, captives adopted into Indian families "are often more brutish, boisterous in their behavior and loose in their manners than the Indians and ... the French who are mixed with the Indians seem also to behave in the like manner."

If Michael La Chauvignerie wound up a prisoner in Philadelphia, the war party that had taken the five Wampler children eventually reached the Allegheny River Valley. The warriors returned to Fort Machault without La Chauvignerie, and his father reported matter of factly to his superiors in Canada "that a party of Indians he had sent out with his son to fight had returned with three prisoners and some scalps, and that his son had gone astray in the woods." The three prisoners presumably were the Wampler children, but what had happened to the other two? Had the warriors given them to the French at Fort Duquesne or to other Indians they met along the way to Ohio? And where had the scalps come from? Michael La Chauvignerie's subsequent accounts of the raid didn't refer to any fighting. Were the scalps that Michael's father mentioned those of the two children who didn't arrive at Fort Machault? That is certainly possible, because detailed descriptions of other raids during the French and Indian War tell of occasional instances in which warriors killed and scalped white children.

After this, the surviving children of Peter Wampler vanish from history. Whether they remained among the Indians or found homes with French families isn't known.

### A Letter in French

Michael La Chauvignerie spent the winter of 1757-58 in Philadelphia as a prisoner of war. Initially incarcerated, he had been released by January 3, 1758, which found him in Germantown and writing to his father. A copy of the letter, which Michael wrote in French, has survived and sheds a little more light on his experiences.

"My dearest father," the teenaged POW wrote. "At the beginning of this new year after having asked for your blessing, I beseech you to grant it to me.

"Allow me also to notify you of my arrival in Pennsylvania. We took five children prisoners, I

33

followed the party for five days. On the fifth, I had the misfortune of losing a flat cake which I had at the bottom of my shirt, which would have served me as food; seeing that I had only that to sustain me, I set out to find it.

"I spent a long time searching for it when suddenly night was falling, and then seeing myself far from the party, I fired two shots, but I had no answer, which made me believe they had taken flight. Believing that the enemy were pursuing me, I was indeed not cautious enough.

"Finally I decided to try to catch up with the party. After three days of walking, seeing that it was impossible to be able to find them again and that I had set about to go on my way to you, I almost lost my life young.

"I considered then that life was dear to me and that it was necessary for me to go where I would be able to save it.

"I arrived at a fort on Oct. 12, 1757, after having gone without food for seven consecutive days. ... Dear father, you can imagine the condition I was in.

"I am in the hands of a good commanding officer who, because of you, has great consideration for me. They shower me with favors, they provide for all my needs. I am very well nourished. They have given me freedom in a little town named Germantown, which is two leagues from Philadelphia where I stayed in prison for two months.

"Dear father, I do not doubt that you treat the prisoners which you have and which you will be able to have well according to their situation. The greatest pains which I suffered are nothing compared to that which you had for me, because I believe that you had no news about my situation and you believed me dead in the forest. But no, I hope to see you again soon because they will exchange us for English prisoners.

"Farewell, my dear father and dear mother. I embrace you with all my heart in the hope of kissing you with tender love, signs of which I will give you for my whole life, be assured of it. I pray you to have the goodness to assure my very humble respects to our nearest relatives.

"With a very deep respect, my dearest father and mother,

"I am your very humble and very submissive and obedient son,

"La Chauvignerie Son."[*]

William Hunter, writing in *Forts on the Pennsylvania Frontier 1753-1758*, reported that Governor Denny in early April sent Job Chilloway, a Delaware Indian, to Venango expressly to deliver a letter written in French. Was the letter the Indian delivered the one that Michael had written to his father? It's possible and even likely, but not certain. At any rate, a transcript, in French, of Michael's letter in French is among the documents appearing in the Pennsylvania Archives for 1758.

Hunter, who cited colonial records, added that La Chauvignerie's stint as a prisoner of war came to an end in late April 1758 when he was exchanged and sent to Hispaniola, a Caribbean island that is one of the Greater Antilles, under a flag of truce. He fades from view after this.

Michael La Chauvignerie's father continued as commandant at Fort Machault. He was still there when a Moravian missionary, Christian Frederick Post, traveled through the region in August 1758. Pennsylvania authorities had sent Post, who had lived among the Indians, to the Ohio country to encourage them to make peace with the English. Post passed but didn't enter the fort at Venango, and Delaware Indian leaders told him that the commander of the small garrison was "an officer blind of one eye."

The French withdrew from the post in mid-1759. As they left, the soldiers set fire to the log fort, which

---

[*] English translation of Michael La Chauvignerie's letter to his father, courtesy of Kathleen A. Szautner, Bethlehem, Pa.

burned to the ground. The English, who had erected Fort Pitt after the French abandoned Fort Duquesne in late 1758, learned of the destruction of Fort Machault from an Indian who came to Fort Pitt in mid-August and delivered "some hatchets picked out of the ruins of Venango."

# Marriage and Love, Frontier Style

*April 1758*

Richard and Catharine Bard lived in a log farmhouse with a thatched roof in the Marsh Creek settlement, west of present-day Gettysburg. The cabin sat at the foot of South Mountain, on the mountain's southeast side, near the creek, which powered the family's sawmill. Richard had piled scrap lumber from the mill at the back of the cabin for use as firewood.

Richard, who was twenty-two, kept a flintlock pistol loaded and hanging on an iron nail he had pounded into a wall of the cabin in case of sudden trouble. The gun must have had a long barrel, because he referred to it as a "horseman's pistol." Bard was more than prudent in taking such a precaution. Only eight days earlier, an Indian war party had attacked the nearby cabin of Thomas and Mary Jameson and

*The Baird (Bard) home and mill on Mount Hope Road, Hamiltonban Township, Adams County, probably taken in the late 1800s.*

*The Taking of Mary Jemison is historical artist Robert Griffing's masterful painting depicting that fateful day in April of 1758. (courtesy of Lord Nelson's Gallery)*

had abducted the Jamesons and four of their six children, along with four members of a neighboring family who had stayed overnight with the Jamesons. The Indians had struck out for Ohio with their ten prisoners. A few days later, a party of frontiersmen, who had attempted to rescue the Jamesons, came upon eight bodies—those of three adults and five children—along the trail. They had been tomahawked and scalped.

As was their custom, the Bards rose early on the morning of Thursday, April 13, 1758. Spring was a busy time on a frontier farm. Among other crops, their farm produced flax, which Catharine spun into linen for use in making homespun cloth. The winter had been mild, and this year spring had come extra early. Richard prepared himself for a hard day's labor, knowing that two young men—Samuel Hunter and Daniel McMenomy—were already at work in his fields. Catharine tended first to their baby, seven-month-old John, and then to the needs of some visitors, who included Richard's cousin, a Pennsylvania soldier named Thomas Potter, and an eleven-year-old girl, Hannah McBride.

The Bards and their guests were unaware of Indian warriors who lurked in the woods little more than three hundred yards away. It was around seven o'clock when Hannah, who had gone outside and was standing in front of the house, saw the Indians approach. The girl "screamed and ran into the house," Bard said later.

Six Indians rushed the house, and several got inside. The warriors "were naked except the breech cloths, leggings, moccasins and caps," Bard said. One warrior carried a large cutlass, which he swung at Thomas Potter. Potter wrested the sword away from the Indian and raised it over his head to swing at the man, but "the point struck the ceiling, which turned the sword so as to cut the Indian's hand" without killing him.

As Potter and the Indian struggled over the sword, Bard grabbed the pistol "and snapped it at the breast of one of the Indians, but ... it did not go off. At this, the Indians, seeing the pistol, ran out of the house."

Bard and Potter rapidly forced the other Indians to leave the cabin, then barred the door from the inside, but more warriors arrived and shoved against the door, which gave way. "The door of the house was thrown down by our pressing to keep the Indians out and their pressing to come in," Bard said. "They shot in the house at us and shot away Thomas Potter's little finger."

Potter and Bard realized that the war party could easily set fire to the house and let the fire force everyone out. The cabin's thatched roof would burn readily, as would the scrap lumber that Bard had piled at the back of the building. The Indians called out in English that they would not kill anyone who surrendered. Considering this, Bard and Potter quickly decided to give up. They surrendered, and the Indians quickly took custody of everybody in the house.

39

There were seven prisoners: Catharine and Richard Bard and their baby; Thomas Potter; Potter's servant, Frederick Ferrick, who was about fourteen years old; nine-year-old William White; and Hannah McBride.

The prisoners stood outside as the warriors plundered the house. One warrior in particular came outside with some of Catharine Bard's clothing, including a petticoat. After looting the cabin, the war party set fire to the mill. The Indians then marched their prisoners in single file toward the woods. They stopped briefly about three hundred yards away from the cabin at a spot where the Indians had left their coats and other gear when they had prepared their assault on the cabin.

"They tied us and took us about 60 rods up the mountain," Bard reported afterward. "Then they brought the two men that had been at work in the field." The war party now had nine prisoners, "and in about half an hour they ordered us to march, setting me foremost of the prisoners. We marched one after another at some distance."

Despite the Indians' promise to spare the prisoners, the warriors soon began killing the captives. "At about seven miles they killed my child, which I discovered by seeing its scalp," Bard said.

The murders had started with that of Thomas Potter, but Richard Bard, walking at the head of the line, had been traveling for several hours before he realized his cousin was dead. "About 12 o'clock I saw another scalp, which I knew to be Thomas Potter's. I have since been informed that they killed him at the place where their match coats lay."

Historian William A. Hunter, giving his source as a letter printed in the *Pennsylvania Gazette* less than a month after the raid, reports in *Forts on the Pennsylvania Frontier 1753-1758* that the war party took its captives past a private defense, Sharp's Fort, and past the ruins of McCord's Fort, which Delaware raiders had captured in April 1756 near present-day Edenville.

The Indians and their surviving captives, now numbering seven, continued traveling into the night. Richard and Catharine Bard told family members years later that after passing McCord's Fort, the war party led them into a gap in the mountain, where they camped for the night. The Bards may not have known it, but the spot was quite close to the place where colonial soldiers had discovered the corpses of the Jameson party the previous week.

### The Second Day

On Friday, April 14 the war party took the trail leading over the mountain and into the Path Valley. "The second day, having passed into the Path Valley, they (the Indians) discovered a party of white men in pursuit of them," the Bards recounted later. "They ordered the prisoners to hasten, for should the whites come up with them, they should all be tomahawked."

(According to Hunter, these pursuers were Pennsylvania soldiers commanded by Captain William Thompson. They belonged to the garrison at Fort

*A full-scale replica of Fort Loudoun has been built on the site of the original fort. It is located near Fort Loudon, Pa. just south of Route 30.*

Loudoun, which Richard Bard's uncle, the late Captain John Potter, had built and commanded in 1756.) The Indians and their prisoners hurried along the path, ascended the Tuscarora Mountain, and succeeded in eluding the soldiers. When they reached the summit, the warriors stopped and let the captives sit down to rest.

The prisoners welcomed the mountaintop respite. Samuel Hunter, who had been one of Bard's farm workers, was sitting next to Bard. Suddenly, "an Indian, without any previous warning, sunk a tomahawk" into Hunter's forehead. The warrior struck him repeatedly, killed him, and then took his scalp.

### The Third Day
On Saturday, April 15 an Indian suddenly daubed red paint on half of Richard Bard's head. Terrified, Bard interpreted this to mean that half the Indians wanted to kill him and half wanted to keep him alive.

### The Fifth Day
By Monday, April 17, the war party had escorted the prisoners across the Sideling Hill and the Allegheny Mountain. The Indian who had assumed custody of Richard Bard had taken to wearing Bard's felt hat, which had a broad brim. While crossing a creek, the wind blew the hat off the Indian's head. The warrior chased it down the creek and retrieved it, but the incident had enraged him. Bard himself had continued crossing the creek, and when the Indian caught up with him, he beat Bard quite severely with a gun. The warrior injured the prisoner so badly that Bard had trouble walking.

Their captors hadn't allowed Richard and Catharine Bard to talk to each other during the past five days, but at camp Monday evening, husband and wife assisted each other in plucking the feathers from a wild turkey that an Indian had shot. Ever so quietly, Richard whispered to Catharine that he intended to escape, and she encouraged him. After supper, the

Indians sat around the campfire. It was roughly ten o'clock—and quite dark—when Richard was sent to a nearby stream to get water. He took a pot that held a quart and slowly walked the fifty-foot distance to the stream. Just then, Catharine caused a commotion. To amuse his friends, one Indian had started to dress in a petticoat he had stolen from her cabin. The others laughed as Catharine challenged him for the garment.

Suddenly an Indian realized that Richard had slipped away in the darkness. "Your man is gone," he shouted. Richard was nearly one hundred yards away from the camp by then. The warriors ran after him, but couldn't catch him. One came back to camp carrying the pot and exclaimed, "Here is the quart, but no man."

### The Fourteenth Day

It took Bard until Wednesday, April 26 to reach safety. Friendly Indians had found him wandering in the forest and took him to a nearby fort. He was nearly dead. When he was revived, Pennsylvania authorities questioned Bard about his experiences, and in making an official statement, he said:

"In nine days and nights, I got to Fort Littleton, having had no food other than four snakes, which I had killed and eaten, and some buds and roots and the like. Three Cherokee Indians (allies of Pennsylvania) found me about two miles from Fort Littleton, cut me a staff and piloted me to the fort.

"In conversation with the Indians during my captivity, they informed me they were all Delawares, for they mostly all spake English. One spake as good English as I can. The captain said he had been at Philadelphia last winter, and another said he had been at Philadelphia about a year ago. I asked them if they were not going to make peace with the English? The captain answered and said they were talking about it when he was in Philadelphia last winter, but he went away and left them."

Some time had passed before Bard had recovered sufficiently from his ordeal to travel to York to make his official statement. In the meantime, Col. George Stevenson reported in a May 7 letter to a colonial official in Philadelphia that:

Richard Beard [sic], who was captivated last month from Marsh Creek, is returned, having made his escape somewhere about the Allegheny Hills. ... He has been so much beat and abused ... that his life is despaired of. Some of them (Bard's captors) told him that they had been lately at Philadelphia, that they would treat with the English as long as they could get presents, and scalp and captivate as long as the French would reward 'em for 'em, that they loved their white brethren so well that they wanted a few of 'em to hoe corn for them, etc., etc.

### A Necklace of Wampum

Although Richard had managed to get back to Pennsylvania, Catharine's ordeal as a captive was just beginning. At some point, a warrior had placed a necklace fashioned of wampum beads around her neck, but didn't say whether it had any significance. As time passed, she grew increasingly fearful that the Indians would eventually murder her.

In late April, the war party reached Fort Duquesne. "After remaining there one night and a day, they went about 20 miles down the Ohio to an Indian town." As she entered the town, an Indian woman took the cap off Catharine's head and began to strike her. Other Native American women joined in, and Catharine was severely beaten. She hardly found the villagers hospitable. Even so, when she learned the war party would soon travel to another town, she didn't want to go. As a relative wrote later, "Now almost exhausted with fatigue, she requested leave to remain at this place, but was told she might, if she preferred being scalped to proceeding. They then took her to a town called Cususkey." This was probably Kuskusky, located at present-day New Castle.

The Indians at Kuskusky abused Catharine and some juvenile captives. When the prisoners were led into the town, many residents turned out to torment them, and they had "their hair pulled, faces scratched and (were) beaten in an unmerciful manner."

It was here that Catharine met a white woman who was also a captive and who had apparently lived among the Delawares for some time. Over the last several weeks, Catharine had seen the Indians kill other prisoners, had herself been threatened with scalping, and had been beaten twice. She confided to the other woman that she feared the Indians intended to kill her eventually. But the other woman, whose name wasn't recorded, replied "that her life was not in danger, 'for that belt of wampum,' said she, 'about your neck is a certain sign that you are intended to an adopted relation.'" In other words, a Native American family intended to adopt her.

The war party took Catharine to still another town, and a chief took her "by the hand and delivered her to two Indian men, to be in the place of a deceased sister. She was put in charge of a squaw in order to be cleanly clothed."

Catharine lived with the Delaware Indians for two years. She refused to learn their language out of fear that if she learned to speak Delaware, she would be forced to marry an Indian man. For all practical purposes, the Indian war ended in the Ohio country in late 1758 when a British army drove the French away from Fort Duquesne and established English control over much of the Ohio River Valley.

### A Matter of Ransom

Richard Bard, fully recovered from his injuries by late 1758, found himself facing a choice. He could make an effort to find Catharine, which would be difficult and perhaps impossible, or he could give her up as lost forever, take another wife, and resume farming. No one would fault him if he did this. The young husband, deciding to rescue her, began a two-year search to find her. He made repeated trips into Western Pennsylvania without locating her. Finally, he offered to ransom her. When he met an Indian who hinted he knew where Catharine was, Richard wrote a letter to her in which he outlined his offer. Somehow he persuaded the Indian to deliver the letter, which instructed Catharine to explain to her adopted family that Richard would pay a ransom of forty pounds for her release.

On a hunch, in the latter part of 1760 Richard decided to travel to Shamokin, along the Susquehanna River where a frontier town was springing up around Fort Augusta. At present-day Sunbury, this settlement was nearly sixty miles north of modern Harrisburg.

As he traveled north, taking an Indian trail along the Susquehanna, "he was met by a party of Indians who were bringing in" his wife. Richard happily gave the Indians the forty pounds. In turn, they handed Catharine to him. Reunited, husband and wife set out for south-central Pennsylvania to rebuild their married life.

But before the Bards departed, Richard told an Indian who had been Catharine's adopted brother that "if he ever came down amongst the white people to call and see him." Some time later, the man, whose name isn't recorded, took the invitation at face value and visited with the Bards, who were then living about ten miles from Chambersburg.

Reunited, Richard and Catharine Bard started a new family and told their offspring stories of the Indian raid on the cabin and the sawmill, the murder of their first-born child, their father's escape, their mother's captivity, and their father's prolonged search for her.

One of their children, a son named Archibald Bard, wrote a lengthy narrative of his parents' ordeals and adventures. Born after his parents were reunited, he drew heavily on the first-hand accounts that his parents had written. His work included a long passage from a poem that Richard wrote in August 1760. The poem reveals that Catharine, or Ketty, was never far

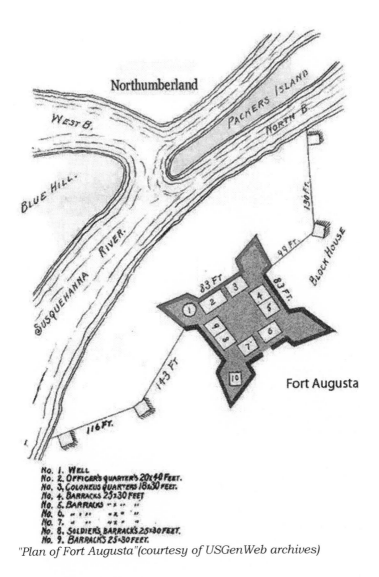

"Plan of Fort Augusta"(courtesy of USGenWeb archives)

from his thoughts. "Alas! Alas! For my poor wife / That's gone to heathen lands," he said in one stanza.

Archibald Loudon included the Bards' story in his 1811 book *Narratives of Outrages Committed by the Indians in The Wars with the White People.*

In the end, Catharine and Richard Bard were buried side by side in a country cemetery near Mercersburg. The region remains quite rural, and a person standing alongside their tombstones today has a clear view of the mountains over which the war party took them nearly 250 years ago.

### Postscript: a Question about Tow

For reasons that aren't clear, Richard Bard kept a small quantity of tow in the pan of the flintlock pistol that he kept loaded and hanging on the wall of his log cabin. Tow was a yellowish fiber left over when farm families processed flax to make linen thread. Women used the thread to make homespun clothes for their families.

To load a flintlock weapon, a man put black gunpowder down the muzzle of the piece, then rammed a lead ball down the muzzle. To fire the gun, he needed to cock the hammer, which contained a specially shaped piece of flint.

Pulling the trigger set off a rapid chain of events: The hammer sprang forward and banged against a strike plate, which was also called a frizzen. This strike produced a shower of sparks, and these ignited a small quantity of gunpowder in the pan. This powder flashed rather than exploded and fire spread through a special vent, or touch hole, in the back of the barrel. This hole led directly to the powder intended to power the bullet. The flash from the pan ignited the charge, which exploded and propelled the ball out of the pistol with deadly force.

On the morning the Indians attacked the Bard cabin, the tow that Richard kept in the pan prevented the pistol from firing.

All this raises a question: Why had Bard placed the tow in the pan of a pistol that he kept loaded and accessible for use in emergencies?

In a 2005 conversation about the Richard Bard case, gunsmith Chuck Dixon of Dixon's Muzzleloading at Kempton, speculated that Bard may have used the tow "to protect the touch hole against insects and moisture" while the pistol hung from the nail on the cabin wall.

Dixon explained that he often advises black powder shooters to put a clean patch in the pan and to close the frizzen. That way, the hunter can walk through the woods or fields with a charged weapon. If he spots a deer, he can quickly cock the hammer, remove the patch from the pan, and put primer in the pan.

Dixon suggested that Bard, in his haste to shoot the Indian rushing him, either forgot or didn't have the time to remove the tow before he pulled the trigger. Hence, the gun didn't fire.

# French Hurriedly Abandon Fort Duquesne

*November 1758*

An army of British regulars augmented by provincial soldiers from Pennsylvania and other English colonies spent the summer and fall of 1758 slowly moving west across the Allegheny Mountains in order to drive the French from the Ohio River Valley. Cherokee and Catawba warriors served as scouts at least part of the time. Brigadier Gen. John Forbes was the commander, but Forbes was seriously ill, and day-to-day command fell to Col. Henry Bouquet, a Swiss soldier who executed the strategies that he and Forbes had planned. The Forbes-Bouquet plan was to march west from Carlisle to the forks of the Ohio at present-day Pittsburgh, constructing a military road and erecting fortifications at regular intervals along the way. Doing this would allow the army to safely move reinforcements and supplies from the eastern settlements to outposts as far west as Pittsburgh.

Early June saw Bouquet in Carlisle, writing dispatches sent to Forbes in Philadelphia or Lancaster. Too ill to ride on a horse, the general traveled most of the way on a litter. The army marched by way of Shippensburg, Chambersburg, Fort Loudon, Burnt Cabins, Littleton, Bedford, Shawnee, Ligonier, Greensburg and, finally, Pittsburgh, where Fort Duquesne stood.

As the British progressed, they not only built new forts, but also strengthened posts erected previously. In 1755 Pennsylvania had cut a road from Fort Loudon to Bedford, and Bouquet had his soldiers improve this road and extend it to west of Ligonier.

*Colonel Henry Bouquet*

Much of it survives today in the form of Route 30 between Bedford and Ligonier.

By mid-October, Bouquet reached the Loyalhanna (or, in the colonel's phrase, Loyal Hannen) Creek, where his men built Fort Ligonier. He began sending out small forces to get information about the situation of the French at Fort Duquesne. Finally, in mid-November 1758, he departed Fort Ligonier, heading northwest toward Fort Duquesne. The colonel fully expected to encounter French forces "and determine by a battle who should possess this country." "We marched from Loyal Hannen with 2,500 picked men without (teams) or baggage, and a light train of

51

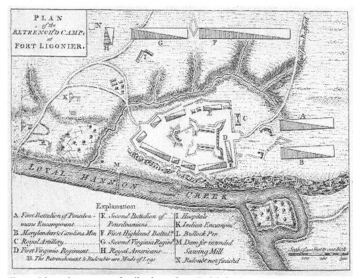

*Fort Ligonier was built by the British in 1758 during the French and Indian War (or Seven Years' War) along the Loyalhanna River in what is now Westmoreland County of southwestern Pennsylvania.*

artillery. ... The distance is about 50 miles, which we marched in five days."

By November 23, the English were about twelve miles east of Fort Duquesne, when Bouquet decided to camp. The army spent November 24 in camp, and Bouquet sent his Indian scouts to the forks of the Ohio. They discovered that the French, clearly aware of Bouquet's approach, had fled. "In the evening, our Indians reported that they had discovered a very thick smoke ... along the Ohio," Bouquet wrote. "A few hours after, they sent word that the enemies had abandoned their fort after having burnt everything."

Bouquet's force arrived at the ruins the next morning. The place was deserted, and the Indian scouts said that some four hundred French soldiers had evacuated the point, mostly by boat, although some had marched away on foot. "They have blown up and destroyed all of their fortifications, houses, ovens

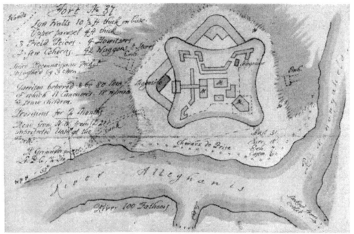

*Watercolor map of Fort Duquesne*

and magazines," the colonel reported. "All the Indian goods (were) burnt in their stores, which seems to have been very considerable."

One hundred French troops descended the Ohio in bateaux; another one hundred crossed the Allegheny and marched overland toward Fort Presque Isle (near present-day Erie) on Lake Erie, and some two hundred sailed upstream to Venango, accompanying the French governor, Francois Le Marchand de Lignery. The French had another post at Venango, Fort Machault, and by November 25, Bouquet had learned that when de Lignery arrived at Venango, "he told the Indians he intended to stay this winter, in intention to dislodge us in the spring."

In their haste to quit the forks, the fleeing French had been unable to demolish Duquesne. "There are, I think, 30 stacks of chimneys standing, the houses all destroyed," wrote one member of the Forbes expedition, whose November 26 letter appeared anonymously in the *Pennsylvania Gazette* on December 14. "They sprung a mine, which ruined one of their magazines. In the other, we found 16 barrels of ammunition, a prodigious quantity of old carriage iron,

*Soldiers march into Fort DuQuesne.*

gun barrels and about a cart load of scalping knives, etc." This writer remarked that the French had departed in a great hurry. "They went off in so much haste that they could not make quite the havoc of their works they intended. ... Whether they buried their cannon in the river or carried them down in their bateaux, we have not yet learned."

With Fort Duquesne aflame, the French withdrew rapidly. "We are told by the Indians that they lay the night before last (November 24) at Beaver Creek, about 40 miles down the Ohio from here," reported the anonymous correspondent.

Their French allies and suppliers gone, the Indians quickly reassessed their situation. "A great many Indians, mostly Delawares, gathered together on the island last night and this morning, to treat with the general, and we are making rafts to bring them over," the man said. (He referred to Smoky Island in the Allegheny across from the fort.)

In June the Rev. Charles C. Beatty, a Presbyterian clergyman who was in his early forties, had been appointed chaplain of Col. John Armstrong's Battalion of the Pennsylvania Regiment. Writing to Bouquet from Carlisle a few weeks after Beatty's appointment, Armstrong had commended him as "a gentleman of strict piety, and extremely zealous for our good cause." The day after the British took possession of the point, Forbes gave the chaplain a special task. "The 26$^{th}$ of this month was observed, by the general's orders, as a day of public thanksgiving to Almighty God for our success," an unidentified member of Bouquet's army reported in a November 28 letter that subsequently appeared in the *Pennsylvania Gazette*. Another correspondent wrote, "Mr. Beatty is appointed to preach a Thanksgiving Sermon for the remarkable superiority of His Majesty's arms."

The troops all knew the story of the British army that had followed Gen. Braddock deep into the wilds of Pennsylvania only to be slaughtered at the Battle of the Monongahela. Some were even survivors of the 1755 expedition. In their victory, Forbes's men were mindful of Braddock's death—and the deaths of hundreds of his soldiers and officers. "Today a great detachment goes to Braddock's field of battle to bury the bones of our slaughtered countrymen," an unidentified member of Bouquet's army reported in a November 28 letter that subsequently appeared in the *Pennsylvania Gazette*. "The French ... have left them lying above the ground ever since."

### December 1758

Winter arrived unseasonably early and caught the English camped out at the forks with little shelter. "We are ... reduced to a sad state of affairs ... with neither tents nor baggage and in need of clothing, with the weather bitter cold (the thermometer at 16 degrees) and getting supplies only with the greatest difficulty,"

Bouquet wrote on December 3. There was one consolation: "the troops are suffering without a murmur, delighted that they have destroyed this nest of pirates, who have cost so much blood."

The British had started to call the place Pittsburgh, and several important chiefs of the Delaware Indians arrived December 4 to meet General Forbes. "The general waited here several days ... expecting to have seen you," Bouquet told them. "But as he was very unwell, he was obliged to set off without having the pleasure to see you."

The Delawares would have to make do with Bouquet as the officer next in command. "I bid you heartily welcome and assure you that I am glad to have the pleasure of seeing you here," he said.

With The Beaver as their speaker, the Delawares had gone to newly named Pittsburgh reluctantly. As Custaloga told Governor de Lignery at Fort Machault a month later, "We were summoned to the forks by an English deputy. ... Forty of us went. Upon our arrival, we were saluted by a volley of artillery and musketry." They had come down the Allegheny's west shore and were reluctant to cross over to the British camp. The English sent an Indian in a boat with "an ox, some flour and a barrel of whiskey. ... As it was already late, we did not want to cross the river until the next day. We were afraid." To test the diplomatic waters, these Delawares sent two representatives over. They came back and reported "that they had been very well received and that the commander asked for at least seven or eight of the principal men. Seven of us crossed the next day. ... We were received at the water's edge by an officer who spoke our language."

As Custaloga told it, the Indians were escorted to the commander's house, and "officers marched before us to keep back the crowd." The Delawares found the colonel "a fine man who, after the most agreeable of receptions, remained standing as he spoke to us." Although the general had waited six days for the delegation to arrive, "he left yesterday because of illness, but he has told me to act as if he were here himself."

Thus begins the Delaware version of Bouquet's remarks, which Captain Andrew Montour, an Iroquois who was the colonel's official interpreter at the meeting, had translated for the chiefs.

According to the official British version, Bouquet stated flatly, "We have not come here to take possession of your hunting country in a hostile manner, as the French did when they came amongst you, but to open a large and extensive trade with you and all the other nations of Indians to the westward ... The general has left here 200 men in order to protect our traders, and I can assure you that as soon as goods can be brought up, you will see a large trade opened for you and all other nations in alliance with you."

Bouquet remarked that his men had come as soldiers, not traders, and consequently had brought no trade goods for the Indians. Even so, "as this is your hunting season, I present you with some powder and lead such as warriors carry and desire your acceptance thereof to kill you some meat for your families."

According to the colonel's version of the meeting, The Beaver expressed approval of Forbe's decision to post two hundred soldiers at the forks. "We assure you it is agreeable to us," The Beaver said, "and we will give them all the assistance we can and give them the earliest notice of any body of the enemy moving this way." This was strategically important because "nobody can come across our country without our knowledge." He cautioned Bouquet to keep his soldiers close to the English camp. "We recommend it to you that none of your people straggle out in the woods as a few Indians may come here and take a scalp without our knowledge."

The Beaver also touched on the delicate subject of white prisoners who had been kidnapped during the war and were living in the Indian towns. "Brother, we

... assure you that you shall see your flesh and blood again, which is in our towns, and that we will use our interest with all other nations to get your people from 'em likewise."

In reporting to the French commander at Fort Machault a month later, Custaloga had a somewhat different understanding of what had been said about the white prisoners. He quoted Bouquet as saying, "I do not speak to you about the English prisoners you have adopted as your relatives and incorporated into your families. I only hope that when peace is made, you will be willing to return those of advanced age, who would be in the way or of very little use to you. As for the young children who are pretty and able to serve you, I will not be angry if they stay among you."

Custaloga added, "The Englishman gave eight large belts, entrusted with clasped hands and peace pipes. ... The Englishman also gave 10 medals struck in Europe, on which a white man and a black man are shown clasping hands."

### The French Account

The French had their own version of their withdrawal from Fort Duquesne.

The Marquis de Vaudreuil had become governor of New France in June 1755. Not quite two months after the destruction of Fort Duquesne, he drew on reports from the Ohio to inform officials in France of the British victory. With a sizeable enemy army steadily advancing, "M. de Lignery saw that there was no longer reason to flatter himself." A withdrawal was inevitable, and he ordered enough provisions for regular and soldiers to last eight days. There were also Indian trade goods to dispose of. "He had the small amount of goods remaining in the King's storehouses packed up and sent to Conchake, (an Indian town near present-day Coshocton, Ohio) for the savages of that village. He appointed a person worthy of trust to distribute the goods and to induce them always take our side and attack the English."

M. de Lignery may have decided to re-establish his command post at Fort Machault on the Allegheny, but he ordered Fort Duquesne's twenty cannons and munitions shipped down the Ohio to French posts in the Illinois country. Subsequently, a score of bateaux departed Duquesne, loaded with artillery and ammunition, accompanied by a hundred soldiers. "There was no other course to be taken in saving them," the governor said. "He also sent to the Illinois the prisoners who were in his possession. This operation was accomplished in less than three hours."

The commandant ordered Fort Duquesne put to the torch. "To blow up the fort, 50 or 60 barrels of spoiled powder were left in the powder magazine," the governor reported.

Nearly all of the French force had left the forks. Many had begun the overland march to Fort Machault, and many others were in boats in the Allegheny. Even at a distance, the explosion was loud. "As soon as M. de Lignery heard the roar of this mine, he sent three men by land to see what damage it had done. They reported that the fort was entirely reduced to ashes and that the enemy would fall heir to nothing but the ironwork of the community buildings."

### A Captive's View

As Dickewamis, white captive Mary Jameson spent the spring and summer of 1758 at the Seneca village at the mouth of Little Beaver Creek. Late that autumn, the French flotilla passed the village as they came downriver with the cannons and munitions they had taken from Fort Duquesne. With winter approaching, the Indians with whom Mary lived loaded their belongings and dried corn onto their horses and into their canoes and descended the Ohio. They stopped and established winter camp at the mouth of the Sciota River. Not only were there plenty of deer and elk, which the men hunted for their meat, but muskrats and beaver were also plentiful, and the hunters trapped them for their furs, which they traded

*Mary Jameson being dressed by the Indians.*

with the whites for firearms, ammunition, and clothing. Mary's Seneca family stayed on the Sciota until spring when "we all returned ... to the mouth of the river Shenanjee, to the houses and fields we had left in the fall before. There we again planted our corn, squashes and beans on the fields that we occupied the preceding summer."

Decades later, Mary Jemison told her biographer, James Seaver, about a day that spring:

About planting time our Indians all went up to Fort Pitt to make peace with the British and took me with them. We landed on the opposite side of the river from the fort, and encamped for the night. Early the next morning, the Indians took me over to the fort to see the white people that were there. It was then that my heart bounded to be liberated from the Indians and to be restored to my friends and my country. The white people were surprised to see me with the Indians ... They asked me my name, where and when I was taken —and appeared very much interested on my behalf. ... My sisters became alarmed, believing that I should be taken from them, hurried me into their canoe and recrossed the river—took their bread out of the fire and fled with me, without stopping till they arrived at the river Shenanjee.

One of her Indian brothers told her later that shortly after she and the Seneca women struck out for the Little Beaver, "the white people came over to take me back." Discovering that she had departed, they made a persistent effort to get the Indians to reveal where she lived. When this failed, they returned to Fort Pitt and in time forgot about her.

As she described this incident sixty-five years later, Mary Jameson reported that during her first year among the Senecas, she had become accustomed to the Indian way of life and had even become "attached to my sisters." Nonetheless, during her brief visit to Fort Pitt "the sight of white people who could speak English inspired me with an unspeakable anxiety to go home with them. My sudden departure and escape from them seemed like a second captivity, and for a long time, I brooded ..."

Mary Jameson, whose surname Seaver spelled Jemison, spent the rest of her life as an Indian.

# Captive Boy Returns to Pennsylvania

*June 1761*

John Mann occupies an obscure niche in the history of the Pennsylvania frontier. He was a child when his mother and uncle took him and his sisters to spend the night of April 4, 1758, in the Buchanan Valley cabin of Thomas and Jane Jameson. The valley was seven or eight miles west of present-day Gettysburg, and Indians raided it at daybreak on April 5. The warriors shot and scalped John's uncle, William Buck, and captured ten people in and around the house. Accompanied by four French soldiers, they took their prisoners along the trail and headed west to the Ohio River. The captives included Thomas and Jane Jameson, four of the six Jameson children, John Mann's mother, whose first name isn't known, John, and his two sisters.

Details of this episode are known only because, in November 1823, James Seaver interviewed the Jamesons' daughter Mary, then eighty. Mary had clear memories of John and his relatives even though "their names I have forgotten." Seaver's biography of Mary included her narrative of the attack and the forced march to the Ohio.

The Indians had rushed the cabin, captured the Jamesons and Manns, looted the cabin, and led the prisoners into the woods. The captives included seven children, four of them quite small. "On our march that day, an Indian went behind us with a whip, with which he frequently lashed the children to make them keep up," Mary said.

The next night an Indian separated Mary, then a girl of fifteen, and John Mann, whom Mary repeatedly described as "the little boy," from the other prisoners, whom they killed and scalped. "A number of times in the night the little boy begged of me earnestly to run away with him and get clear of the Indians." But Mary refused. "I told him that I would not go, and persuaded him to lie still." Her advice probably saved their lives. Had they attempted to escape, these Indians, who were skilled trackers, would likely have recaptured them and killed them. Even if they had managed to elude the Indians, their chances of survival in the forest would have been slim.

A few nights later, John and Mary watched in horror as the warriors sat around the campfire and dried and painted the scalps of their relatives. Mary said later that she and John could tell "by the color of the hair" whose scalps they were.

Several days west of the Pennsylvania settlements, the Indians encountered a second group of warriors, going toward Ohio with one prisoner. Mary described him as "a young white man who was very tired and dejected. His name I have forgotten."

The two groups headed west together, and nine days after the raid on the Jameson cabin, the war parties reached Fort Duquesne. As they approached the fort, "the Indians combed the hair of the young man, the boy and myself, and then they painted our faces and hair red in the finest Indian style."

Mary and the two boys were "conducted into the fort, where we received a little bread, and were then shut up and left to tarry alone through the night," Mary said. When morning arrived, "our masters came early and let us out of the house and gave the young man and boy to the French, who immediately took them away. Their fate I have never learned, as I have not seen or heard from them since."

The fate of the young man who was the prisoner of the second war party remains a mystery, but a little is known about the fate of the Mann boy. To begin with, a newspaper account published within weeks of the attack on the Jameson cabin identified his uncle as a frontiersman named Robert Buck. The article also noted that Buck's sister-in-law, her two daughters, and son were the wife and children of William Mann, a Pennsylvania Regiment soldier stationed at Carlisle, forty miles to the north.

Three years later, the French and Indian War was over, and the commander of British troops in North America was Gen. Jeffrey Amherst. In June 1761, when Amherst was in Albany, NY, he sent a letter to the governor of Pennsylvania that included a list of white prisoners that the French and Indians had surrendered. Here is the text of the document, which was sent as an enclosure:

"Return of English children, delivered up by the Indians and Canadians, that were taken in the Province of Pennsylvania and Colony of Virginia.

1. "Nicholas Silvias, of Plowpark, in Pennsylvania, taken in 1755 by Indians.
2. "John Mann, of Marsh Creek, in Pennsylvania, taken in 1758, by Indians.
3. "Frederick Payer, of Low Bergen, in Pennsylvania, taken in 1756. His father killed, but his mother, he believes, is still living.
4. "Anne Coon, of Pennsylvania. Her mother dead, and her father was taken at the same time.
5. "Isaac Toople, taken near Presque Isle in 1756. (Presque Isle is a peninsula in Lake Erie.)
6. "Mary Williams, daughter to one Daniel Williams, taken by Indians on the Delaware about five years ago, believes her father and mother were killed.
7. "Peter Dawson, of Virginia, taken in 1755 near the Ohio.
8. "Richard Underwood, taken about Winchester, belongs to Virginia."

The general noted that he had intended to send a ninth youngster, a boy named James Cristis, with this group, but had changed his mind when it turned out—

*Gen. Jeffrey Amherst*

if a bit belatedly—that he had been taken from the Mohawk River Valley in the New York Colony.

The general's letter to Gov. James Hamilton in Philadelphia reported that "among the children lately sent from Canada ... I find that there are six that were taken in the government of Pennsylvania and two in Virginia." Amherst added that the enclosure accompanying the letter "contains all the intelligence I can give you of them."

65

He assigned a man to escort the children on a boat trip down the Hudson River. The boat was to land at Amboy (present-day Perth Amboy, N.J., across from Staten Island in New York Harbor) and the children were to travel across New Jersey to Philadelphia. It wasn't clear whether they were to walk or go by coach.

Five weeks later the general sent a second letter to Governor Hamilton, this one dated July 23:

"Sir, I am this day favored with your letter ... by which I have the pleasure to learn that the children returned from captivity in Canada, which I directed to be delivered over to you, had arrived safe and were, except two (presumably, the Virginians), already restored to their friends, for which care and intelligence I return you many thanks."

After Amherst's brief mention, John Mann disappears from view.

# 'Little Bear Woman' Recalls Pennsylvania Childhood

*November 1778*

In January 1835, an Indian trader named Colonel George W. Ewing was traveling along the Mississinewa River, a tributary of the Wabash that joins the Wabash at Peru, a city in northern Indiana. Established around 1825, Peru was then a small town. The Mississinewa Valley was the country of the Miami Indians, and at The Deaf Man's Village, he stayed overnight in the cabin of a Native American family. As the evening wore on, he engaged an elderly woman living there in a lengthy conversation. The woman was Maconaquah, or Little Bear Woman, and she was the widow of Shepconnah, a war chief who had established Deaf Man's trading post after he lost his hearing. To Ewing's surprise, she told him that she had been the child of a white family back in Pennsylvania and that an Indian war party had stolen her when she was a little child. Her father had been a settler named Slocum.

Ewing soon returned to his home in nearby Loganport, Indiana, and wrote a detailed account of the woman in a letter, dated Janua 20, 1835, which he mailed to the U.S. postmaster at Lancaster, Pennsylvania.

"There is now living near this place," Ewing wrote, "an aged white woman, who a few days ago told me, while I lodged in the camp one night, that she was taken away from her father's house, on or near the Susquehanna River, when she was very young—say, from five to eight years old, as she thinks—by the Delaware Indians, who were then hostile toward the whites."

*Colonel George W. Ewing*

Ewing reported the old woman had told him that she had lived most of her life as an Indian and that she didn't remember much of her pre-Indian childhood. Nonetheless, she did retain some vivid memories of her life in Pennsylvania. For instance, she said that her father "was a Quaker, rather small in stature, and wore a large-brimmed hat; was of sandy hair and light complexion, and much freckled; that he lived about half a mile from a town where there was a fort; that they lived in a wooden house of two stories high, and had a spring near the house."

The woman provided some specific details of the Slocum family. "She says her father had a large family, say eight children in all—six older than herself, one younger, as well as she can recollect."

Ewing said that the elderly woman had described her kidnapping. "She says three Delawares came to the house in the daytime, when all were absent but herself, and perhaps two other children: her father and brothers were absent making hay in the fields. The Indians carried her off, and she was adopted into a family of Delawares, who raised her and treated her as their own child."

The woman had married a Miami Indian "by whom she had four children; two of them are now living— they are both daughters and she lives with them. Her husband is dead; she is old and feeble, and thinks she will not live long."

Ewing explained she hadn't ever told anyone the story of her life "fearing that her kindred would come and force her away" from her Indian family. "She has entirely lost her mother tongue, and speaks only in Indian, which I also understand, and she gave me a full history of herself."

She was vague about many aspects of her Pennsylvania childhood. "Her own Christian name she has forgotten, but says her father's name was Slocum ... She also recollects that it was upon the Susquehanna River that they lived, but don't [sic] recollect the name of the town near which they lived. I have thought that from this letter you might cause something to be inserted in the newspapers of your country that might possibly catch the eye of some of the descendants of the Slocum family, who have knowledge of a girl having been carried off by the Indians some 70 years ago."

Ewing offered to take relatives of the woman to see her.

The Lancaster, Pa., postmaster who received Ewing's letter, Mrs. Mary Dickson, appears to have placed the letter in a stack of papers, where it remained for more than two years. As it happened, in 1837, the letter passed into the hands of John Forney, the new editor of a local newspaper, the *Intelligencer*. He read and published it. One of his readers was a clergyman, the Rev. Samuel Bowman, who had once lived in Wilkes-Barre and had known a family named Slocum. Family members had often talked about a little girl, Frances, whom Indian warriors had stolen during the Revolutionary War. No sooner had Bowman read Ewing's letter than he sent a copy of the *Intelligencer* to the Slocums of Wilkes-Barre.

Soon after, Jonathan J. Slocum, Esq., an attorney who was a nephew of the kidnapped child, wrote to Ewing. "An aunt of mine—sister of my father—was taken away when five years old by the Indians, and since then we have only had vague and indistinct rumors upon the subject. Your letter we deem to have entirely revealed the whole matter, and set every thing at rest. ... Steps will be taken immediately to investigate the matter, and we will endeavor to do all in our power to restore a lost relative who has been 60 years in Indian bondage."

That was in early August 1837. Ewing replied that he would gladly assist the Slocums. By August 26, he reported that he had determined the old woman was still alive. He explained that although he would be away from Loganport for an extended period of time, he would arrange for a man he trusted to take the Slocums to The Deaf Man's Village if they arrived in

*Frances Slocum captured by Indians at age 5*

Indiana in his absence. This man would be James T. Miller, who lived near Loganport in the small town of Peru. Miller "knows her well," Ewing said. "He is a young man whom we have raised. He speaks the Miami tongue, and will accompany you if I should not be at home." The woman and her family lived along "the Mississinewa River, about 10 miles above its mouth," he said.

Three Slocum siblings, although elderly themselves, quickly organized an expedition to Indiana in September. One brother, Isaac, had moved to Ohio, and he hurried to Peru and arranged for James Miller to take him to see the old woman. She received him politely, but without a visible display of emotion or enthusiasm. Isaac, then sixty-two, had been three when his sister was kidnapped. He had been too young to remember much, if anything, of the episode, but he knew the family story that when Frances was a child, one of her older brothers, Ebenezer, a boy of about ten, had smashed her finger with a hammer while the children played in their father's blacksmith shop. Isaac remembered this anecdote when he noticed that the forefinger of the old woman's left hand was disfigured.

JOHN L. MOORE

He asked how she had injured her finger. When Miller had translated his question, she replied in an Indian language and Miller interpreted her response: "My brother struck it with a hammer in the shop, a long time ago, before I was carried away."

This answer quickly convinced Isaac that the woman was his sister. He went back to Peru and awaited the arrival of his brother Joseph, who was sixty-one, and his sister Mary, who was sixty-nine. It was early autumn when the Slocum siblings, accompanied by Miller the interpreter, approached the log house where their sister lived. Nearly fifty-nine years had passed since the war party had attacked their home and taken the girl.

### Family Reunion

The travelers arrived in The Deaf Man's Village on September 22, 1837. The old woman greeted them politely but without enthusiasm.

The travelers learned that the child they had known as Frances had become the sixty-four-year-old Indian grandmother known as Ma-co-na-quah, a name that meant Little Bear Woman. They had little difficulty in proving to her that she was their sister. Even so, she remained emotionally distant from them. They asked if she remembered the name she had had as a little girl.

"It is a long time," she said. "I do not know."

"Was it Frances?" one of the Slocums asked.

Maconaquah thought, then said, "Yes. Franca. Franca."

The visit was cordial and lasted several days. The Slocums made a written record of some of the questions they asked Maconaquah, as well as a transcript of her responses.

Q. "Were you ever tired of living with the Indians?"

A. "No; I always had enough to live on, and have lived well. The Indians always used me kindly."

Q. "Did you know that you had white relations who were seeking you for so many years?"

*Frances Slocum – Ma-Con-A-Qua*

A. "No; no one told me, and I never heard of it. I never thought anything about my white relations unless it was a little while after I was taken."

Her sister and brothers invited her to join them in Pennsylvania.

Q. "We live where our father and mother used to live, on the banks of the beautiful Susquehanna, and we want you to return with us; we will give you of our property, and you shall be one of us, and share all that we have. You shall have a good house, and every thing you desire. Oh, do go back with us!"

A. "No, I can not. I have always lived with the Indians; they have always used me very kindly; I am used to them. The Great Spirit has always allowed me to live with them, and I wish to live and die with them. Your wah-puh-mone (looking-glass) may be longer than mine, but this is my home. I do not wish to live any better, or anywhere else, and I think the Great Spirit has permitted me to live so long because I have always lived with the Indians. I should have died sooner if I had left them. My husband and my boys are buried here, and I can not leave them. On his dying day my husband charged me not to leave the Indians. I have a house and large lands, two daughters, a son-in-law, three grandchildren, and every thing to make me comfortable. ..."

Mary, Joseph, and Isaac related their account of the day the war party attacked the Slocum farm and took Frances. As the Indians rushed in, her older sister grabbed her baby brother and ran off. Mary said that she was the girl who carried the baby to safety, and Joseph, who was sixty-one, said he had been the baby.

### Maconaquah's Account

Maconaquah gave this account of her memory of that day:

"I can well remember the day when the Delaware Indians came suddenly to our house. I remember that they killed and scalped a man near the door, taking the scalp with them. They then pushed the boy through the door; he came to me and we both went and hid under the staircase. They went up stairs and rifled the house, though I cannot remember what they took, except some loaf sugar and some bundles. I remember that they took me and the boy on their backs through the bushes. I believe the rest of the family had fled, except my mother.

"They carried us a long way, as it seemed to me, to a cave, where they had left their blankets and traveling things. It was over the mountain and a long way down on the other side. Here they stopped while it was yet light, and there we stayed all night. I can remember nothing about that night, except that I was very tired, and lay down on the ground and cried till I was asleep.

"The next day we set out and traveled many days in the woods before we came to a village of Indians. When we stopped at night, the Indians would cut down a few boughs of hemlock on which to sleep, and then make up a great fire of logs at their feet, which lasted all night. When they cooked anything, they stuck a stick in it and held it to the fire as long as they chose. They drank at the brooks and springs, and for me they made a little cup of white birch bark, out of which I drank. ...

"Very early one morning two of the same Indians took a horse, and placed the boy and me upon it, and again set out on their journey. One went before on foot, and the other behind, driving the horse. In this way, we traveled a long way till we came to a village where these Indians belonged. I now found that one of them was a Delaware chief by the name of Tuck Horse. ...

"Early one morning this Tuck Horse came and took me and dressed my hair in the Indian way, and painted my face and skin. He then dressed me in beautiful wampum beads, and made me look, as I thought, very fine. I was much pleased with the beautiful wampum. We then lived on a hill, and I remember he took me by the hand and led me down to the river side to a house where lived an old man and woman."

These people had had children, but all were gone. "I was brought to these old people to have them adopt me if they would ... They agreed to it, and ... they gave me the name of We-let-a-wash, which was the name of their youngest child, whom they had lately buried."

### A Second Visit

In 1839 Joseph Slocum made a second trip to Indiana to visit his sister. This time his two daughters went along, and one, Hannah Bennett, kept a journal. One entry provides a description of her aunt:

[who] is of small stature, not very much bent; had her hair clubbed behind in calico, tied with worsted ferret. Her hair is somewhat gray, her eyes a bright chestnut, clear and sprightly for one of her age, her face is very much wrinkled and weather-beaten. She has a scar on her left cheek, received at an Indian dance. Her skin is not as dark as you would expect from her age and constant exposure. Her teeth are remarkably good. Her dress was a blue calico short gown, a white Mackinaw blanket, somewhat soiled by constant wear, a fold of blue broadcloth lapped around her, red cloth leggings, and buckskin moccasins.

Bennett also described her aunt's dwelling:

She said she is able to have a better house, but fears to do it on account of the jealousy of the Indians. She has money; some that has been saved since the treaty of St. Mary's, 18 years ago. ... They had cloths and calicoes enough to fill a country store. They have a looking-glass and several splint-bottomed chairs. A great many trinkets hang about the house, beads and chains of silver and polished steel. Some of their dresses are richly ornamented with silver brooches, seven or eight rows of brooches as closely as they can be put together. They have many silver earrings. My aunt had seven pairs in her ears; her daughters perhaps a dozen apiece. They have saddles and bridles of the most costly kind, six men's saddles and one side-saddle. They have between 50 and 60 horses, 100 hogs, 17 head of cattle, also geese and chickens. Their house is enclosed with a common worm fence, with some outhouses, principally built of logs. A never-failing spring of excellent water is near the door, with a house over it.

As the Miami Indian woman called Maconaquah, Frances Slocum lived with her Indian family for the rest of her life. She never returned to Pennsylvania, not even for a visit. She was seventy-four years old when she died in March 1847. She was buried near her cabin in her family's cemetery, alongside her husband, Shepconnah, and sons.

Her name and story live on. In Pennsylvania, a state park located about ten miles northwest of Wilkes-Barre is Frances Slocum State Park. Local tradition asserts that she spent her first night in captivity in a rock shelter on a hillside that is now part of the park. The rock shelter is a natural feature formed by a massive rock that juts out from the hillside and creates a high ceiling over a relatively flat surface large enough to accommodate several adults and children who are sitting or lying down.

In Indiana, the U.S. Army Corps of Engineers has dammed a section of the Mississinewa River near Peru to create Mississinewa Lake, which provides both flood control and recreation. A lakeside trail is called the Frances Slocum Trail. The Frances Slocum State Forest, also in Indiana, is situated along the Mississinewa between the dam and Peru.

Writers have long been fascinated by the story of Frances and the decades-long effort that her Pennsylvania family made to find her. Over time, a number of books have been written about her. One of them was *Biography of Frances Slocum, The Lost Sister of Wyoming* that Pennsylvania author John F. Meginness published in 1891. This article is based on that book.

# Frontier Ordeals Live on as Family Stories

*Post-1800*

Indian raids were frequently so dramatic that within days after they occurred, colorful accounts about them spread along the frontier. Sometimes they reached the ears of colonial officials who wrote them down and included them in their official reports to their superiors.

Timothy Horsfield, the Pennsylvania magistrate at Bethlehem, did just that in a November 30, 1756, letter to Gov. William Denny. Horsfield detailed an attack that had happened two days earlier—on the evening of Sunday, November 28—at a cabin in the Allemengel section in what is now the southern section of Schuylkill County and the northern part of Berks. The magistrate informed the governor that the man making the report was "John Holder (who) came here this evening from Allemengel." Horsfield assured Denny that Holder insisted that he had obtained the story from credible sources, who weren't identified. But Holder offered plenty of information about the attack.

According to Horsfield's report to the governor: The cabin belonged to a settler named Schlosser. As evening came on, there were a number of people in the cabin, and someone closed and barred the door. Suddenly there was a knock on the door.

"Who is there?" Schlosser or another occupant asked, suddenly wary.

"A good friend," a male voice replied from the outside.

This response wasn't persuasive, and nobody opened the door.

The people inside the cabin again asked, "Who is there?"

This time there was no response. After a tense moment, curiosity got the better of one of the men. His name was Stonebrook, and he looked out of the window. That was a fatal error because "an Indian discharged a gun and killed him on the spot," Holder told Horsfield.

The settlers became panicky when Stonebrook collapsed on the cabin floor and died. Someone opened the door, and a woman and her two daughters, attempting to escape, ran outside. But "the Indians pursued and took both the children," Holder said.

A man at the cabin shot the warrior who had grabbed the girls. Wounded, he fell down and let go of the children. One girl ran off, but the Indians caught the second girl and took her away. The wounded Indian "cried out very much, but in a short time he got up and made off," Holder said.

**Unexpected Dinner Guests**

Pioneer families that survived Indian attacks and captives who were reunited with their families told and retold stories of their experiences. These tales were handed down over generations. Sometimes the mere appearance of peaceful Indian men in a frontier settlement was enough to frighten the white people— and create a memorable event. It took nearly half a century for one such tale to be written down, and thus preserved. Drawing on a childhood memory, Archibald Loudon recounted in his 1811 book, *Narratives of Outrages Committed by the Indians in The Wars with the White People,* how, in 1765, he and his siblings had been outside their house in a valley near the Tuscarora Mountain. It was late morning on a Sunday when they saw "three Indians coming across the meadow. ... We ran into the house and informed our parents, who were considerably alarmed." Carrying guns, the strangers approached the house. When they seemed peaceable, his father invited them inside for a meal. Decades later, Loudon remembered that before the Indians went inside, they "set their guns down on the outside of the house. ... After taking dinner they sat a considerable time." One man "could speak tolerable good English," but the other two "spoke nothing ... but Indian or something that we could not understand."

The visitors appeared friendly enough, but the Loudon family experienced a tense moment when one of the children, apparently curious about the Indians, walked over to them. The child was "one of my sisters, a child of three or four years old, having very white curly hair." The whiteness of the girl's hair fascinated the Indians, whose own hair was black. "They took hold of her hair between their finger and thumb, stretching it up and laughing."

The Loudon family feared for the worst and read sinister meanings into the Indians' conversation, which they could not understand.

"'This,' we conjectured they were saying, 'would make a nice scalp, or that they had seen such,'" Loudon wrote. The family relaxed when they realized that their guests meant no harm. "After some time ... we saw they had no hostile intentions."

The Indians stayed for about two hours, then continued their journey. A few days later the Loudons learned that one of their visitors had been Captain John Logan, a well-known Iroquois chief who was one of Shikellamy's sons. Logan had lived in the Susquehanna River Valley for many years, but eventually moved to what has become West Virginia and settled in the Ohio River Valley. "He was a remarkable tall man," Archibald Loudon said forty-five years later, "considerably above six feet high, strong and well proportioned."

About a decade after his unscheduled visit with the Loudon family, Chief Logan took up the hatchet, went on the war path and took the scalps of thirteen white men. The Indian leader was sufficiently important and

*Photographic reproduction of a print depicting James Logan (1725-1780), a chief of the Mingo tribe.*

spoke so eloquently that Thomas Jefferson once compared him to some of the world's greatest orators.

### Stuck Family Massacre

Families that suffered losses during the Indian wars took pains to pass down both oral and written accounts of their adventures. The neighborhood of the Snyder County village of Salem, a hamlet a few miles northwest of Selinsgrove, was the setting of two Indian raids that occurred during the Revolutionary War.

Members of the Stock/Stuck family, many of whom now live in the Central Susquehanna Valley, notably in Northumberland and Snyder Counties, retain both oral and written accounts of a 1781 raid in which Indians from western New York killed several family members. An important version of the episode and its aftermath came from an elderly man who lived near Salem in the 1890s. Some of his ancestors had been neighbors of a family known variously as the Stocks or the Stucks, and had provided their descendants a detailed verbal account of what had happened to them. Late in the nineteenth century, when the Pennsylvania State Government established an official commission to determine the locations of frontier forts erected during the French and Indian War and the American Revolution, the old man shared his story with one of the commission's researchers, and his detailed description of the incident made its way into the commission's two-volume, official report.

Responsible for tracking down information about colonial and Revolutionary War era forts in Pennsylvania's Juniata and Cumberland Valleys, a Middleburg historian named Jay Gilfillan Weiser enlisted a number of heritage-minded people to assist him. One of them was a Snyder County lawyer, William K. Miller, Esq., who lived in Salem. Miller documented the history of Hendrick's Fort, a log blockhouse erected over a spring, circa 1770. It had stood, Weiser reported, "within a stone's throw of the public road leading from Selinsgrove to Lewistown." This road appears to have passed through Salem.

One of William Miller's sources was Matthias Dauberman, who had spent his entire life in the vicinity of Salem. Aged seventy-five, he retained a vivid account of the raid on the Stock/Stuck family, which he inherited from his great-grandparents, who had lived about a quarter mile away from the Stuck cabin. Dauberman said that his version of the raid had come from his grandfather, who had been a boy of about five.

"The men were in the fields at work when some Indians who had been lurking in the woods nearby swooped down upon the small log house and attacked the defenseless women and children," Dauberman said.

The septuagenarian told Miller, "They killed outright old Mrs. Stuck and two of the children and also a man who happened to be near. They then dragged away with them young Mrs. Stuck, wife of one of the Stuck boys. She was so much terrified with what she had beheld that she fainted when but a short distance from the house and, after reaching the woods beyond the cleared fields, they dragged her a considerable distance into the thicket, where the Indians killed and scalped her."

With four scalps in hand, the Indians withdrew quickly and headed north toward New York State. The killings outraged people in the neighborhood, and they enlisted the services of three men—Grove, Pence, and Stroh—who had had experience in fighting Indians and who lived in what is now Shamokin Dam. Led by these three, the settlers "followed the fleeing savages," Dauberman recalled. "They were captured in the course of a few days while sitting about their fire in the forest, having made off in the direction of the New York border. ... All who are supposed to have had a hand in this butchery were killed by the Indian fighters ... and the settlers who were with them."

It apparently took some time for the settlers to realize that the raiding party had murdered Mrs. Stuck in the woods nearby. "Mr. Dauberman relates that he heard his grandfather state that the body of young Mrs. Stuck, who was dragged into the woods, was not discovered until some days afterwards." The woman's remains were recovered and given proper burial, although Weiser's account doesn't say where.

Weiser and Miller, who were friends, felt sufficiently comfortable with the old man's version of events for Weiser to include it in copious detail in his December 14, 1894, report to the commission. Weiser noted that at the time Miller interviewed him, Dauberman was "tall and vigorous in frame, with a ruddy countenance and a memory as bright and keen as we might expect to find." Thus a family story carried down for four generations found its way into the official "Report of the Commission to Locate the Site of the Frontier Forts of Pennsylvania."

### A Graveyard Rhyme

Not far from the site of the Stuck farm, a monument stands in a cemetery alongside an old church in Salem. It memorializes George Row, an eighteenth century settler in his late fifties who lived in a log cabin several hundred yards north of the church. Local tradition has it that Row was coming home from a mill when a war party surprised him. His log home survives, and his descendants still talk about him. An inscription on the tombstone, written in English, tersely notes that Row was "killed by Indians 1780." A longer inscription, this one in German, contains a verse, which, translated into English, says:

> *The Death certain*
> *Uncertain the day*
> *The hour is, too.*
> *No one knowing may*
> *Therefore fear**

---

*English translation courtesy of Johann Szautner.

# Pipes of Peace,
# Pipes of War

*Tobacco*
"An Indian carries pouch and pipe with him wherever he goes, for they are inseparable," according to David Zeisberger, a Moravian missionary and woodsman who lived with the Delawares and other Indians for more than six decades. "In the pouches they carry tobacco, fire materials, knife and pipe."

Pipes and the tobacco that Native Americans smoked in them were basic to many aspects of Indian life. They were important in making peace as well as in making war. References to tobacco and pipes abound in the literature of the Eastern Frontier.

Zeisberger spoke several Indian languages, knew their cultures and history, and recorded many details in his diaries and manuscripts. Native smokers, he said, frequently mixed sumac with tobacco. "Few can stand smoking pure tobacco."

Tobacco had ceremonial, social, and religious uses. It was often grown and dried by Indian women, who sometimes smoked it. Individual Indians were fond of smoking tobacco recreationally. Sacrificing small amounts at an appropriate time might bring a hunter good luck. "If an Indian hunter hears an owl screech in the night, he immediately throws some tobacco into the fire, muttering a few words at the same time. Then they promise themselves success for the next day for the owl is said to be a powerful spirit," reported Zeisberger, writing in 1779 and 1780 about the Indians living in Pennsylvania, New York, and Ohio.

But tobacco figures in the historical record perhaps most prominently because of the role it played in times of war and times of peace. Native smokers

85

*David Zeisberger*

made pipes of clay, but they often used finely carved pipes fashioned from special materials such as slate, soapstone, serpentine, and catlinite to smoke tobacco during special ceremonies and rituals.

Zeisberger said that the Delawares traded with the Cherokee Indians to obtain pipes made from a hard white stone—"probably white marble"—and painted black. "These pipes are made so neatly that they are no heavier than the European pipes," the missionary wrote. Also, Indians returning from the Mississippi River Valley occasionally brought pieces of red marble, which they carved into pipes. "Such pipes, however, are as a rule to be seen only in the possession of chiefs or captains, for not many of them are to be had."

The chronicler said that the use of a fine pipe of this sort was generally reserved for councils and other solemn occasions. "This is carried about by the chief counselor, each one present draws a few whiffs of smoke, and this is called, 'smoking the peace pipe.'"

John Heckewelder, a Moravian colleague of Zeisberger who also lived with the Delaware Indians for several decades during the late 1700s, reported that the Delawares employed a special tobacco pipe when performing what he termed "peace errands."

"The pipe of peace, being either made of a black or red stone, must also be whitened before it is produced and smoked out of on such occasions," the missionary said. To whiten a pipe, "it must be daubed all over with chalk, white clay or anything which changes the color from black to white," Heckewelder said.

Indians whom Heckewelder knew in the Ohio country told legends of what life had been like for Native Americans before Europeans arrived during the 1500s and 1600s: "We and our kindred tribes lived in peace and harmony with each other ..." They lived in a huge region that "extended far to the north and far to the south. In the middle of it, we would meet from all parts to smoke the pipe of peace together."

If Indians smoked tobacco when making and celebrating peace, they also used it when planning for

*John Heckewelder.*

war. Zeisberger, for instance, offered this detailed account of how Indian leaders used tobacco to recruit fighters when organizing a war party: "Captains, when about to go to war, send to the captains of the nation or towns who are in league with them, a piece of tobacco to smoke, thus notifying them that they themselves will soon follow. By this they intend that the captains shall smoke their pipes and consider seriously whether they will take part in the war or not.

One chief about to visit another will similarly send him a piece of tobacco to smoke with the message that he smoke, look in a certain direction and in due time he will see the sender coming."

Heckewelder gave a similar report: "A black (wampum) belt with the mark of a hatchet made on it with red paint is a war belt, which, when sent to a nation together with a twist or roll of tobacco, is an invitation to join in a war. If the nation so invited smokes of this tobacco, and say it smokes well, they have given their consent and are from that moment allies."

The literature of the eastern frontier contains many references to tobacco. The following passages, arranged chronologically, offer a sampling of the uses of tobacco and related paraphernalia.

### 1608: Along Chesapeake Bay

The summer of 1608, Captain John Smith, who was based in Jamestown, Va., was exploring the upper section of the Chesapeake Bay when he encountered a group of some sixty Susquehannock Indians. They had heard of his arrival near the mouth of the Susquehanna River and "came down with presents of venison, tobacco pipes, baskets, targets, bows and arrows," Smith reported. One man carried a tobacco pipe that Smith described as "three quarters of a yard long, prettily carved with a bird" at one end. Other Indians brought pipes with carvings of deer or bear. To the Englishman, the ends of these pipes appeared strong enough to "beat out the brains of a man."

### 1609: Off the Coast of New Jersey

Henry Hudson was an English navigator who explored for Holland on a ship called *The Half Moon.* He sailed into New York Harbor in late summer, 1609. Crew member Robert Juet, in his diary entry for September 4, wrote that "the people of the country came aboard of us, seeming very glad of our coming."

The natives brought green tobacco and swapped it for beads and knives.

### 1616: Western New York

In 1616 the French adventurer Etienne Brule had been traveling with a war party of Susquehannock Indians on a mission against the Iroquois. Brule got separated from them and wandered through the forest for several days without eating. Desperate for food, he approached some Iroquois fishermen who fed him, smoked a pipe, and took him to their village "where they entertained him."

### 1631: Delaware

In 1631 Dutch colonists established a small settlement, called Swannendael, on Cape Henlopen in present-day Delaware. Their mission was to raise crops and catch whales. Someone erected a wood post and on it placed the Coat of Arms of Holland, which was painted on a piece of tin. An Indian from the neighborhood stole the tin and used it to make some tobacco pipes. This angered the colonists, who protested vigorously to the Indian leaders. To mollify the Europeans, the chiefs executed the Indian, but the Dutch, far from being placated, admonished the Indians and said they had overreacted. Embittered, the Indians soon after massacred the colonists.

### 1638: on the Delaware River

Europeans were quick to notice the native fondness for pipes and soon began giving pipes made in Europe to the Indians as gifts. In July 1638, for instance, an English seaman, Captain Thomas Yong, sailed up the Delaware River. When a party of Susquehannock Indians, also called Minquas, traveling in a canoe saw the sails on his ship, they made a beeline for it.

"The Minquas rowed directly to my ship," Yong said, "and as soon as they got near her, they made signs for a rope, which was cast out to them." The

Indians tied their canoe to the ship and clambered aboard. Through Yong's interpreter, they said they wanted to see what the captain had to trade. "I used them courteously," Yong said, "and gave them each a hatchet, a pipe, a knife and a pair of scissors."

### 1743: Shamokin

In April 1743 Conrad Weiser visited Shamokin, an Indian town in Central Pennsylvania, just as Shikellamy was returning from Onondaga, the Six Nations capital in western New York. The chief brought an official message from the Iroquois council intended for the governors of Pennsylvania and Virginia, but directed to the Delawares and Shawnee as well. The previous year, some white Virginia frontiersmen had attacked and killed members of an Iroquois war party en route to the Carolinas on a raid against the Catawba Indians. The dead included a cousin of Shikellamy. Many Iroquois warriors had wanted to avenge the killings, which had been unprovoked, but Shikellamy said that the Iroquois chiefs, rather than risk a border war with the English colonies, had decided to let the governor of Pennsylvania mediate on their behalf with his counterpart in Virginia. "We have ordered our warriors with our strongest words to sit down and not to revenge themselves," Shikellamy told an open council in Shamokin.

Olumapies, the Delaware chief at Shamokin who was also known as Sassoonan, said later that he liked the Iroquois decision, because his people lived midway between Virginia and Iroquois country. Indian war parties heading for Virginia and armed Virginians heading for western New York would "both ... pass through the place of his residence (and) a state of war would be very disagreeable to him."

When the council ended, Shikellamy saw that his family provided "a handsome Indian dinner ... to all that were present," Weiser said. Weiser himself made a speech after dinner in which he conveyed the news that the governor of Virginia was looking for "an amicable way" to resolve the matter with the Iroquois. After that, Weiser "presented the company with two rolls of tobacco ... to smoke while they were in company together, to talk about the good news they had heard that day, according to the custom of the Indians."

### 1743: Onondaga

In the summer of 1743, Conrad Weiser and Shikellamy traveled to Onondaga. Colonial authorities had sent Weiser and Shikellamy to encourage the Iroquois leaders to suppress the fighting against the Catawbas and other southern Indians.

Weiser, who kept detailed notes about the trip, reported that he and Shikellamy arrived in Onondaga (present-day Syracuse, N.Y.) on July 21 and explained that they had brought a message to the Iroquois from the governor of Pennsylvania on behalf of the governor of Virginia. The Iroquois greeted the messengers warmly, and one, showing considerable hospitality, invited them to stay at his house.

"After we had eat(en) some dried eels boiled in hominy, and some mats had been spread for us to lie upon, Canassatego and Caheshcarowanoto of the chiefs, with several more, came to see us and received us very kindly," Weiser wrote. The Indians asked about the governor and other people they had met in Pennsylvania. "We smoked a pipe of Philadelphia tobacco together and had some further discourse on things of no consequence," he said.

### 1755: Penns Creek

Early in the morning of October 16, 1755, a war party attacked farmers living along the Penns Creek near present-day Mifflinburg. As the raid progressed, two Indians appeared at the cabin of a farmer named Leininger, who was in the house, along with a son and two daughters. "They demanded rum, but there was none in the house," daughter Barbara reported later. "Then they called for tobacco, which was given them.

Having filled and smoked a pipe, they said, 'We are Allegheny Indians and your enemies. You must all die!'"

They shot and killed Barbara's father and fatally tomahawked her brother, who was twenty. Then they forced Barbara and her younger sister, Regina, to accompany them into the forest. Each girl spent several years as an Indian captive.

### 1756: Fort Augusta

Accompanied by small numbers of French soldiers, Delaware raiding parties struck white settlements all along the Pennsylvania frontier during the spring and summer of 1756. Responding to a request from the Six Nations, in June the Pennsylvania Regiment sent a battalion of troops up the Susquehanna River and in early July started construction of a large stockade post, Fort Augusta, at the confluence of the west and north branches. Even as construction progressed on this defense, hostile Delawares led by Captain Jacobs besieged Fort Granville on the Juniata River near present-day Lewistown. The garrison surrendered after the Indians set fire to the log fort, and the warriors took their prisoners to Kittanning, a large Delaware Indian town on the Allegheny River. On September. 8 Pennsylvania soldiers attacked Kittanning at dawn, destroyed much of the town, and killed Captain Jacobs.

Ogaghradarisha, a Six Nations chief loyal to Pennsylvania, had been in the Delaware town at Tioga, high up on the Susquehanna's North Branch at modern Athens, in early October 1756. Two Delaware Indians came to Tioga with news that the English had destroyed Kittanning "and that the Ohio Indians and several other tribes to the number of one thousand were collected at Fort Duquesne, and that the French were preparing themselves to march in a very short time with them on a design to lay siege to" Fort Augusta.

Hearing this, Ogaghradarisha decided to descend the river and warn the garrison at Fort Augusta, where he arrived on October 11. His journey to Shamokin had been an eventful one. "Two days ago," an officer wrote in an official report, "as he was coming down the river, he saw a great number of Delaware Indians and conversed with one of their chiefs, who told him that he had promised to meet the governor of Pennsylvania at Bethlehem and to take with him all the Delaware tribe on Susquehanna, and that they were going on that design. But that another of the chiefs gave him a piece of tobacco covered over with vermilion (a scarlet red) and desired him to smoke it, which he with scorn refused to do, and returned it to him, telling him at the same time that the English were his best friends and that he would never consent to shed the least drop of their blood."

# Selected Bibliography

Bouquet, Henry. *The Papers of Henry Bouquet*. vol. II: The Forbes Expedition Edited by S. K. Stevens, Donald H. Kent and Autumn L. Leonard. Harrisburg, Pa.: The Pennsylvania Historical and Museum Commission, 1951.

*Colonial Records*. vol. VII. Harrisburg, Pa.: Theo. Fenn & Co., 1851.

Heckewelder, John Gottlieb Ernestus. *An Account of the History, Manners, and Customs of the Indian Nations, Who Once Inhabited Pennsylvania and the Neighboring States*. Philadelphia: Publication Fund of the Historical Society of Pennsylvania, 1876. (Reprint edition by Arno Press Inc., 1971)

Hunter, William A. *Forts of the Pennsylvania Frontier, 1753-1758*. Harrisburg: Pennsylvania Historical and Museum Commission, 1960.

Loudon, Archibald. *A Selection of Some of the Most Interesting Narratives of Outrages Committed by the Indians in Their Wars with the White People*. 1808-1811, vols. I and II. Carlisle, Pa.: The Press of A. Loudon, 1811. (Reprint edition by Garland Publishing Inc., 1977.)

Meginness, John F. *Biography of Frances Slocum, The Lost Sister of Wyoming*. Williamsport, Pa.: Heller Bros. Printing House, 1891.

*Pennsylvania Archives*, First Series. vols. I and II. Edited by Samuel Hazard. Philadelphia: Joseph Severns & Co., 1853.

Rupp, I.D. *History of the Counties of Berks and Lebanon*. Lancaster, Pa.: G. Hills, 1844.

Seaver, James. *A Narrative of the Life of Mrs. Mary Jemison.* Canandaigua, N.Y.: J. D. Beamis and Co., 1824. (Reprint edition by Garland Publishing Inc., New York, 1977.)

Swift, Robert B. *The Mid-Appalachian Frontier: A Guide to Historic Sites of the French and Indian War.* Gettysburg, Pa.: Thomas Publications, 2001.

Wallace, Paul A.W. *Conrad Weiser, 1696-1760: Friend of Colonist and Mohawk.* Philadelphia: University of Pennsylvania Press, 1945.

Wallace, Paul A.W. *Indian Paths of Pennsylvania.* Harrisburg: Pennsylvania Historical and Museum Commission, 1971.

Zeisberger, David. *David Zeisberger's History of North American Indians.* Edited by Archer Butler Hulbert and William Nathaniel Schwarze. Columbus, Ohio: Press of F.J. Heer, 1910.

Made in the USA
Middletown, DE
11 June 2018